THE ENEMY OF *Marriage*

FATAI KASALI

THE ENEMY OF MARRIAGE

Copyright © 2015 Fatai Kasali

The author has asserted his right to be identified as the author of this work in accordance with the Copyright, Designs and Patents Act 1988.

All rights reserved. No part of this publication may be reproduced, stored in a retrieval system, or transmitted, in any form or by any means, electronic, mechanical, photocopying, recording or otherwise without the prior permission of the author.

All Scripture quotations, unless otherwise indicated, are taken from the Holy Bible, King James Version, Cambridge University Press, Oxford University Press, Harper Collins and the Queen's Printers.

Published in the United Kingdom by Glory Publishing

ISBN: 978-0-9926138-6-0

Acknowledgements

To God be the glory for the grace to write this book. I give God all the praise and adoration for giving me the inspiration through His Spirit. This has made possible the writing of this book.

My wife, Felicia Ebunlomo, gave me priceless support during the writing of this book. My two sons, Daniel and David, have been very supportive.

To all those who have contributed one way or the other to the beauty of this work, thank you very much. May God Almighty bless you all.

Contents

	Introduction	7
1:	In the Beginning	9
2:	Operations of Satan	25
3:	The Power of Knowledge	53
4:	Pressure at Home	71
5:	The Spirit of Individualism	81
6:	Attack on Communication	89
7:	Strife	105
8:	Co-operative Faith	117
9:	Jezebel Spirit	125
10:	Spiritual Warfare in Marriage	141
11:	Brokenness	161

Introduction

"*Now the serpent was more subtil than any beast of the field which the LORD God had made. And he said unto the woman, Yea, hath God said, Ye shall not eat of every tree of the garden?*"
Genesis 3:1

In the beginning, Satan lured Adam and Eve into disobedience. Satan hates marriage, and the first satanic attack recorded in the Bible was against this first holy couple. He made them both sin against God. Since then, Satan has been working against the success of marriage. He has explored many different avenues to create trouble in marriage. He uses the weaknesses of the partners to cause crises in their marriage.

For you to be able to solve your marital crisis, you will need to identify the involvement of Satan. For your marriage to stand, you will need to be conscious of Satan. Satan is the real enemy of marriage; it is not your spouse or any other human being. The weaknesses in your spouse or yourself might have given opportunity to Satan to get involved in the affairs of your home, but you must understand that the real enemy of your home is Satan.

This book will educate you about the different kind of avenues Satan exploits to cause marriage crises. You will learn how Satan exploits the moral weaknesses of the partners to create troubles in their relationship. You will also discover through this book, how to close the door of your home against Satan – the real enemy of marriage.

Every chapter in this book has prayer points that will bless you.

I pray in Jesus' name that your home will be glorious and that every attack of Satan against your marriage shall fail.

1

In the Beginning

"*And he answered and said unto them, Have ye not read, that he which made them at the beginning made them male and female, And said, For this cause shall a man leave father and mother, and shall cleave to his wife: and they twain shall be one flesh?*"

Matthew 19:4-5

"*And the LORD God said, it is not good that the man should be alone; I will make him an help meet for him. And out of the ground the LORD God formed every beast of the field, and every fowl of the air; and brought them unto Adam to see what he would call them: and whatsoever Adam called every living creature that was the name thereof. And Adam gave names to all cattle, and to the fowl of the air, and to every beast of the field; but for Adam there was not found an help meet for him. And the LORD God caused a deep sleep to fall upon Adam, and he slept: and he took one of his ribs, and closed up the flesh instead thereof; And the rib, which the LORD God had taken from man, made he a woman, and brought her unto the man. And Adam said, this is now bone of my bones, and flesh of my flesh: she shall be called Woman, because she was taken out of Man. Therefore shall a man leave his father and his mother, and shall cleave unto his wife: and they shall be one flesh. And they were both naked, the man and his wife, and were not ashamed.*"

Genesis 2:18-25

Marriage was established by God at the beginning of creation. God put the first couple in the Garden of Eden, which He gave to them as a home. But He didn't leave them on their own: He also related with them regularly. God visited Adam and Eve in the Garden of Eden to speak with them. This is clearly revealed in the second and third chapters of the book of Genesis, in the Bible.

From that first marriage in the Garden of Eden, the following information can be deduced:

1. GOD IS THE AUTHOR OF MARRIAGE

It was God who laid the foundation for marriage. He saw the need for a wife in Adam's life. Because God is the author of marriage, therefore, any idea, principle, doctrine or philosophy that will be applied to marriage must come from God. Only God has the knowledge that can make marriage work. Whatever does not agree with the Word of God should not be applied to marriage.

2. GOD HAD A PURPOSE FOR ESTABLISHING MARRIAGE

God wanted to give Adam a helper that would be suitable for his destiny. God also wanted Man to procreate—spread and multiply on the earth. You need to ask yourself about your purpose for getting married. This will help you to avoid abusing your partner. Where the purpose is not known, abuse is inevitable. Do you see your partner as a helper in your destiny? Do you see yourself and your partner as having a common destiny to fulfil? If you have married your partner for a selfish purpose that will not fulfil the purpose of God, then you need to repent and seek the face of God for mercy.

3. ACCEPTANCE IS MANDATORY IF MARRIAGE IS TO BE SUCCESSFUL

God brought Eve to Adam as a helper but He did not force Adam to marry her. God allowed Adam to make his own decision about Eve. Adam then said, *"This is now bone of my bones…, she shall be called Woman…" (Genesis 2:23)*. This is evidence of acceptance. You must accept your spouse and everything about him/her. You must accept his/her height, body shape, family background, etc. Some of the signs of lack of acceptance in marriage include incessant complaining and criticism, irritation, avoidance, individualism, etc. The person you accept will always be without fault to you. Because neither you nor your partner is an angel, there may be certain weaknesses in both of you, but that does not affect acceptance. With love, you can talk through any personal weakness and help each other to become better in your relationship.

4. THERE MUST BE CLEAVING TOGETHER

Genesis 2:28 says that a man must leave his parents and be joined to his wife. That is, there must be some sort of separation from relatives and close associates if marriage is going to be successful. You must be emotionally separated from certain people in your life and be totally joined to your spouse. Parents can offer advice, but they must not have any control over your marriage. Your spouse must be your confidante, closest associate, partner in all things, and best friend. Your spouse must be the one who knows everything about you – not any other person.

5. SPOUSES MUST BE PROUD OF EACH OTHER IN ALL SITUATIONS

In *Genesis 2*, Adam and Eve were both naked and not ashamed. You must never be ashamed of your spouse. You must always be proud of your spouse in all situations. Never spread a bad report around about your spouse. Maintain integrity and the honour of your home. Avoid telling people, including your parents, negative things about your spouse. If you need counselling, find a credible, independent counsellor and avoid destroying the reputation of your home. Complaining to other people about your spouse's shortcomings will never solve your marital problems, and will most likely make them worse.

6. Marriage is for Mature People

Genesis chapter 2 states that a man will be joined to his wife. This implies that marriage is between a man and a woman, not a boy and a girl. There are heavy responsibilities involved in marriage and it is only mature people who can handle them. Nevertheless, it should be mentioned that age does not necessarily indicate maturity. It is possible to be elderly and still lack the necessary wisdom. Therefore, maturity will require a person who can function in a position of power, leadership, authority and influence. It will also involve somebody who can take responsibility for his/her actions. The mature person must also be matured in words, perception, understanding, thoughts and actions. A mature person must be independent of parents and able to live an independent life.

7. Marriage will Require Openness of Heart

Genesis 2 states that Adam and Eve were naked and not ashamed. That is, they were open to each other. For your marriage to be successful, you will need to be open with each other. There should be no hidden agenda, no secrecy. Openness builds up unity in the home. It is difficult to be one with somebody when you know little about his or her life.

8. There are Differences Between a Man and a Woman

Adam was called a man while Eve was called a woman – because they are different. Man is naturally more aggressive because he is a hunter, given the responsibility of hunting for food for his family. Man is built with muscles and aggression to help him capture food and serve his family well. He occupies the position of a problem solver and every member of the family looks toward him for a solution to their problems.

A woman must understand that a man is naturally built to be more aggressive and able to defend his family. Even a regenerated man still exhibits a degree of aggressiveness in many situations. There are chemicals and hormones inside a man that make him behave in a certain way that is different to a woman.

Similarly, there are certain hormones and chemicals inside a woman that influence her emotionally. Some of these chemicals are produced in the body of a woman periodically, while some are continually being secreted. These chemicals enable a woman to be a woman in terms of pregnancy, breastfeeding, menstruation, etc. All these affect the mood of a woman regularly and occasionally.

A man must know that there are clear differences between the way a woman and a man will react under the same circumstances, irrespective of the level of spirituality. This is because the chemical compositions are not the same. When your wife comes under the influence of emotion, you should not personalise it. It is not about you, but what makes her a woman.

9. God united the two, male and female, by an indissoluble bond in the marriage of one man to one woman

There was no possibility of separation because the bond between the two was indissoluble. Similarly, there was no possibility of adultery because this would require disunity in the marriage for it to happen. That unity was of God, and not of man.

10. It was two lives joined into one

There were no individualistic statements like, "I have got my life to live." The two lived the same life. They had the same vision, dreams and goals to pursue. They had only one plan. They walked together, lived together, and did all things in common. They did not live an independent life.

11. THE TWO PARTNERS WERE YOKED TOGETHER

This made it impossible for one to cheat the other. They were one, closely united, and pulling equally together in all the concerns of life. They fought battles of life together. The two partners worked equally to make the marriage work. The struggle of one becomes the struggle of both.

12. THE PARTNERS HAD ONLY ONE SOURCE: GOD

God was the only counsellor they had. God was the only helper they had. God was the only one they consulted in all things. God occupied the central position in their relationship.

13. THERE WAS NO THIRD PARTY

The only friend they had was God. The bond between them was so strong that it couldn't accommodate any third party, except God who made the bond.

14. THERE WAS NO STRUGGLE

This is because there was no lack of provision and they also shared all things together. They never fought over material things. They never fought over possessions. There was no competition at home.

15. THEY HAD NO KNOWLEDGE OF EVIL

They did not see any evil in each other. They never suspected each other. They did not imagine or expect evil from each other. They only thought good of each other. Their love was sincere. There was no doubt in the relationship.

16. THEY CONTINUALLY LIVED IN THE PRESENCE OF GOD

They lived where God put them. They carried out the tasks God gave them. They never pursued their own purposes. They experienced fullness of joy. This is because in the presence of God, there is fullness of joy. They never had any reason to weep. It was joy galore in the Garden of Eden: there was no sickness, no failure, and no death. It was a perfect environment.

So what went wrong?

The devil came to lure them into disobedience. It should be borne in mind that Adam and Eve never disobeyed God before Satan showed up in their relationship. The major problem for this couple was that they only knew God. They did not know that there was somebody called the devil. So, when he came to them, they innocently welcomed him and gave him an audience. They were so naive and innocent that they treated the devil as if everybody was as good as God. They did not even know that evil exists.

For your marriage to succeed, you must know that there is somebody called the devil. You must know that Satan exists and his mission is to turn man against God. It is also part of his mission to destroy whatever God has made, because he hates God and all His works. There is a devil, and there are demons---the ministers of the devil. There are also wicked human beings who have given themselves to the devil to be used by him for his destructive missions.

Furthermore, instead of seeking clarification from God about this devil who they knew nothing about, they started dealing with him. When you come across a strange situation in your marriage, you must consult God first for clarification. Seek God in all your confusion and uncertainties. Do not handle strange situations that come against your marriage by yourself.

The first satanic operation against humanity was recorded in the book of Genesis, chapter three. This attack was against a married couple. The devil understands that if he can succeed in destroying marriage, the whole creation will experience its negative consequences.

And still today, the attack of Satan against marriage rages on. Hell is busy mapping out diverse strategies to destroy marriage, so that God's purposes for it will suffer. Many homes are destroyed today due to satanic attack. There are so many former partners that have become enemies due to satanic operations.

As I said before, it is significant that Adam and Eve never had a problem with God until Satan showed up. The same is true today. Without satanic involvement in the affairs of the home, marriages will fulfil the purpose of God. After the fall of Man in the Garden of Eden, men became enemies of God in all things. Due to the fact that Adam and Eve listened to Satan in the beginning, men still listen to Satan today. There is a lot of collaboration going on in many homes between partners and Satan, without the partners knowing.

If Adam and Eve had not listened to Satan, it would have been impossible for him to destroy their relationship with God. The same principle is still valid today. One or both of the partners will need to listen to Satan for him to carry out his mission in their homes. Naturally, nobody would decide to listen to Satan if they realised it was happening, but it takes place in a subtle ways.

Lessons from Eden

"Now the serpent was more subtil than any beast of the field which the LORD God had made. And he said unto the woman, Yea, hath God said, Ye shall not eat of every tree of the garden? And the woman said unto the serpent, We may eat of the fruit of the trees of the garden: But of the fruit of the tree which is in the midst of the garden, God hath said, Ye shall not eat of it, neither shall ye touch it, lest ye die. And the serpent said unto the woman, Ye shall not surely die: For God doth know that in the day ye eat

thereof, then your eyes shall be opened, and ye shall be as gods, knowing good and evil. And when the woman saw that the tree was good for food, and that it was pleasant to the eyes, and a tree to be desired to make one wise, she took of the fruit thereof, and did eat, and gave also unto her husband with her; and he did eat. And the eyes of them both were opened, and they knew that they were naked; and they sewed fig leaves together, and made themselves aprons. And they heard the voice of the LORD God walking in the garden in the cool of the day: and Adam and his wife hid themselves from the presence of the LORD God amongst the trees of the garden. And the LORD God called unto Adam, and said unto him, Where art thou? And he said, I heard thy voice in the garden, and I was afraid, because I was naked; and I hid myself. And he said, Who told thee that thou wast naked? Hast thou eaten of the tree, whereof I commanded thee that thou shouldest not eat? And the man said, The woman whom thou gavest to be with me, she gave me of the tree, and I did eat. And the LORD God said unto the woman, What is this that thou hast done? And the woman said, The serpent beguiled me, and I did eat."

Genesis 3:1-13

These verses show the first satanic operation against humanity as recorded in the Bible. The story of this event in the Garden of Eden is still relevant today. Satan is still busy plotting the downfall of many homes. The following lessons can be deduced from the satanic attack against the marriage of Adam and Eve:

1. BE AWARE YOU ARE BEING WATCHED

Satan knew about the discussion that took place between Adam and God. They never invited Satan, but he came on his own. He had no doubt been watching them for a long time, looking for the best opportunity to strike.

Adam and Eve never knew that somebody was watching them. You must know that people around you are watching the events going on in your marriage. That is why you must not be careless with your relationship. There are eyes focusing on and observing what is going on in your home. Satan could possess any of these evil observers to manipulate your marriage.

Such people may come with knowledge they have collected from what they see and observe in your relationship. Such intruders talk with authority and confidence to lure you into releasing more information into their hands. They are workers of iniquity. They will soon use the information collected from you against your marriage.

2. Maintain Consistent Intimacy at Home

Either Satan came to Eve when Adam was not around, or Adam decided to remain passive in the conversation between Eve and Satan. You will never know when the enemy of your marriage intends to strike. You must remain 'glued' to your spouse always. Avoid 'on and off' intimacy. God has called couples into consistent – not occasional – intimacy.

3. Maintain a Certain Level of Secrecy About Your Home

Eve exposed her home to Satan and the devil manipulated the situation. Eve did not know the intention of the devil who was asking her the questions, and yet she shared with him, the instruction they had received from God. There are some things that should not be shared with everybody. Releasing confidential information about your home to an outsider may expose your home to satanic attack. What people do not know can't influence them. Some friends or relatives cannot handle certain information. If you relay it to them, Satan will manipulate it in their mind and use them against you. Do not forget that envy has been the root of most household wickedness.

4. Control Your Knowledge

God did not want Adam and Eve to eat the forbidden fruit because they would have the knowledge of good and evil. After the fall, Adam saw Eve as the root cause of his disobedience.

They started seeing evil in each other.

There is some information you will have that could make you start seeing evil in your spouse. It is a result of the fallen nature of man. It was not like that in the beginning. Avoid incessant criticism of your spouse; otherwise this will open a door to Satan manipulating your thinking towards your spouse. Avoid fault-finding in your spouse. Focus on the good things about your spouse. Too much attention given to the faults of your spouse will expose your thinking to satanic manipulation of your reasoning and actions towards your spouse.

Evil knowledge about your spouse may make you see evil in him/her all the time. Control your knowledge about your spouse, otherwise it will control you. Do not let negative things you know about your spouse be the dominant factor that controls your attitude towards him/her.

5. GET YOUR FACTS RIGHT

Eve misquoted God. In *Genesis 2:17*, God did not say that they should not touch the fruit in the Garden, only that they must not eat it. Yet in *Genesis 3:3*, Eve adds, *"Neither shall ye touch it..."* Do not talk about what you are not sure of; it can lead you into error. Misinformation will expose you to Satan's manipulation. Many homes have been destroyed today because of misinformation. Do not act on anything unless you are certain about it, otherwise you may destroy your home out of ignorance. Practice good communication in your home.

6. CONTROL YOUR AMBITION

Adam and Eve ate the fruit because they thought it would make them like God. Unfortunately for them, they ended up becoming like Satan – the author of disobedience. Do not let ambition tear your home apart. There are some ambitions that will expose you to satanic manipulation, which may threaten the survival of your marriage. Avoid excessive ambition. Be aware that any vision or dream you develop that threatens the existence of your marriage can never be of God.

7. Rule Over Your Sight

In *Genesis 3:6*, forbidden fruit looked pleasant to the eyes of Adam and Eve. But when they ate it, it turned them into the enemy of God. Not everything that looks pleasant is beneficial. Some things look good but are not godly. Let the Spirit of God lead you, not your sight.

8. Some Mistakes Can Become Generational

Through the disobedience of Adam and Eve, all of humanity has suffered. The spiritual 'gene' of disobedience entered into the bloodstream of Man. Today, everyone who is born inherits the seed of disobedience. Be aware that your action of today can determine your children's destiny. Do not let Satan manipulate you into wrongs that will destroy a future generation – your children. Think deep before you act. Your actions have direct consequences on your children – for good or evil.

9. Some Damages Are Irreparable

There are certain things that, if lost, can never be recovered. Adam and Eve never regained the Garden of Eden. They lost it permanently. Be careful of the way you live. There are some mistakes that can't be corrected. Sins may be forgiven, but some of them have consequences that cannot be reversed. Avoid exposing yourself to error.

10. Know Your Threats

It is your responsibility to identify what threatens your marriage. God did not educate Adam and Eve about Satan. They were to discover him and put him where he belongs. They failed to do this, and suffered for it. Similarly, God has placed some responsibilities in your hands.

The reason why God gives you His Word (the Bible) is to make you wise, so that you can be in control of your circumstances – to a certain extent. You must explore your environment and identify things that can threaten your home and deal with them accordingly. God will not do everything for you; neither will He tell you everything. You need to explore your surroundings and identify your threats before it is too late. The threat you leave unattended may become an instrument in the hand of Satan to use against your marriage.

11. Avoid Misuse of Unity

Adam and Eve lived a life of unity. They were one in their actions. They were one in disobedience to God. They jointly ate the forbidden fruit. Neither questioned the other. It sounds good to always be united, but make sure you're united on the right things. If not, it could expose your home to satanic manipulation. There is a boundary for everything in life. It is a misuse of unity to disobey God together. Do not follow your spouse in breaking one of God's instructions. Do not sacrifice obedience for the sake of unity.

12. You are Individually Responsible for your Actions as a Couple

You may agree to sin together as a couple, but punishment will come to the individual. All the excuses of Adam and Eve did not hold water. They tried to avoid responsibility for their sinful action, but God held them accountable individually. The curse of Adam differs from that of Eve. If you allow your spouse to lead you to sin against God, you are still responsible for your own action.

13. Outside Can Affect Inside

THE ENEMY OF Marriage

What you do outside your marital home can seriously affect your marriage. Eve held a discussion with Satan, an outsider, and her marriage suffered for it. You must control all your external involvements to safeguard your marriage.

Prayer

Every foundation for marital failure operating against my home – Father, scatter it today in Jesus' name.

In the name of Jesus, Father, overthrow today any evil agent assigned against my marriage.

Any association that myself or my partner is involved in, that will damage my home, may the Holy Spirit's power take us out of it today, in Jesus' name.

Father, arise and overthrow any giant standing against peace and unity in my marriage, in the name of Jesus.

Father, cause any evil power assigned to oppress your purpose for my home to fail, in Jesus' name.

You, arrow of marital storm, be diverted away from my home and return to your sender, in Jesus' name.

I decree that the spirit of hatred and strife shall fail over my marriage, in Jesus' name.

In the name of Jesus, I command any source sending a water of trouble into any area of my marriage to dry up now.

I decree, in the name of Jesus, that any power, agent, spirit or personality that sponsors disunity shall not succeed over my home.

I terminate any and every demonic influence over any matter that concerns my home, in the name of Jesus.

2

Operations of Satan

Satan is a spirit being. He has demons as servants. Through his demons, Satan is able to carry out many evil operations. In some situations, Satan can possess a human being to use as his agent to carry out his destructive mission in the life of his target.

Understanding how Satan operates will make you wiser and more able to detect when he is at work on your marriage. You will also be able to know if you have opened a door for satanic influence on the affairs of your home. Usually, Satan will need at least one of the partners to cooperate with him and listen to his evil counsel, in order to succeed in destroying their relationship.

Satan's mission

Satan is on a mission against mankind. His mission is a three-fold one, as stated in *John 10:10*:

"The thief cometh not, but for to steal, and to kill, and to destroy: I am come that they might have life, and that they might have it more abundantly."

The three aspects of Satan's mission are: "to steal, to kill, and to destroy."

Satan is a thief. He steals people's blessings. He can steal (take away forcefully) our joy, peace, prosperity and every manner of blessings. When he is allowed to operate in a relationship, he can create issues that will enable him to take your joy, peace, sound mind and every other blessing in that relationship. Many couples have unknowingly lost their joy to Satan.

Satan is a killer. He is able to bring an end to the life of a relationship. He can terminate the existence of a home. He can cause a marriage to end beyond restoration.

Satan is a destroyer. He can destroy peaceful co-existence in a place. He can make two people who used to call each other 'my love' into two people who hate each other with a passion. You must fight Satan, this master of destruction, with all your might and never allow him entrance into your home. If Satan is allowed into a place, he can do unimaginable damage.

Satan achieves his mission in different ways. Some of his methods include the following:

1. HE TRANSFORMS HIMSELF

"Satan himself is transformed into an angel of light."

2 Corinthians 11:14

Satan is able to appear as an angel of light. He has the ability to seem good in order to gain entrance into a place and carry out his destructive mission. He can influence the mind of a person with evil counsel, by making it appear good. You should not be too quick to follow any counsel or engage in a situation that appears good to you, especially when you face a marital crisis.

Also, don't be too quick to welcome an adviser who appears to be caring about your marriage. Satan can pretend to be caring and loving. Be wise.

2. HE IS AN EXPLOITER

"Lest Satan should get an advantage of us..."

2 Corinthians 2:11.

Satan knows how to exploit the prevailing situation to achieve his destructive mission. He is able to take advantage of the present crisis in a relationship to make things worse.

For example, a couple maybe having a minor argument about parenting and if they are not careful, Satan will exploit the situation to drag them into a greater crisis. The couple may unwittingly move from the issue of parenting they are discussing into accusing each other in a derogatory way. From this matter, they move on into certain issues of the past. The situation can become complicated and they may start fighting each other. They will no longer be talking about parenting, but irrelevant issues of the past. Satan has exploited the parenting issue to drag them into a more volatile matter, capable of luring the partners into a wrong action.

Satan is clever in taking advantage of situations. He is able to exploit the weaknesses of the partners to lure them into a marital crisis.

3. HE IS A SCHEMER

"...for we are not ignorant of his devices."

2 Corinthians 2:11

Satan has schemes, plans and devices. He will use any kind of trick, technique or malign means to serve a particular purpose or plan to succeed in one of his evil tasks. Satan can invent an untrue story to set partners against each other. He can generate evil dreams to create confusion in a marriage. He can bring an evil report upon a

THE ENEMY OF Marriage

partner to create strife in the relationship. The prime motive is to cause division and hinder the success of the marriage.

You should not be too quick to believe bad things you hear about your partner, irrespective of who told you. You must prayerfully consider it before drawing a conclusion. Satan can raise people to speak his word into a relationship. Be wise.

4. HE CAN MOMENTARILY USE THE MIND OF A PERSON

Satan is able to speak into the mind of a person. This is possible because man has a physical body, 'the flesh', which is an open door to whatever is contrary to the things of the Spirit of God.

"He saith unto them, But whom say ye that I am? And Simon Peter answered and said, Thou art the Christ, the Son of the living God. And Jesus answered and said unto him, Blessed art thou, Simon Barjona: for flesh and blood hath not revealed it unto thee, but my Father which is in heaven."

Matthew 16:15-17

In the above story, the Spirit of God spoke through Peter to give the appropriate answer to the question Jesus asked. This is commendable. But wait a minute, read the story further:

"Then Peter took him, and began to rebuke him, saying, Be it far from thee, Lord: this shall not be unto thee. But he turned, and said unto Peter, Get thee behind me, Satan: thou art an offence unto me: for thou savourest not the things that be of God, but those that be of men."

Matthew 16:22-23

In the above story, the same Peter who earlier spoke spiritually now spoke fleshly. Satan put an evil word into the mind of Peter. The switch from spiritual to flesh was very quick. Do not be too quick to believe every thought that comes into your mind, because Satan can speak his word into your mind to lure you into the destruction of your marriage.

Similarly, do not be too quick to react to wrong words your partner says to you. It could be that your partner was not speaking his own word but that of Satan. Soon, your partner may come back to his or her senses and regret what was said. Satan can speak into the mind of a man or woman, irrespective of the level of their spirituality, even if just for a moment. Remember, every human being is made of flesh, which is frail.

5. SATAN CAN ENTER INTO A PERSON

"Then entered Satan into Judas surnamed Iscariot, being of the number of the twelve."

Luke 22:3

That is, Satan exerted a strong influence over Judas, and incited him to betray Jesus. After Satan gained entrance into Judas, he came into full control of his thoughts, imagination and actions. Before this happened, Mathew 26:14-16 records how Judas met with those who wanted to arrest Jesus. He took money from them as payment to betray Jesus.

It is also recorded in *John 12:6* that Judas was a thief. This implies that Judas, however unknowingly, actually gave himself up to Satan to use. Every bad habit that you refuse to repent from will open a door to satanic invasion into your life, to be used for an evil assignment.

For example, through anger, some partners have been used by Satan to destroy their marriages. Through greed, some partners have been used by Satan to abandon their homes and run after fake promises from evil people. If there is any bad habit in you, drop it now before Satan invades you to destroy your marriage. Remember, when Satan succeeds in taking over a man, the man will lose control of himself during that time, until the evil operation

THE ENEMY OF *Marriage*

is complete. There are people that show regret for a past action, though during the time of the deed, they thought they were in control of themselves.

6. SATAN CAN TURN A PERSON INTO A DECEIVER

"But Peter said, Ananias, why hath Satan filled thine heart to lie to the Holy Ghost, and to keep back part of the price of the land? Whiles it remained, was it not thine own? And after it was sold, was it not in thine own power? Why hast thou conceived this thing in thine heart? Thou hast not lied unto men, but unto God. And Ananias hearing these words fell down, and gave up the ghost: and great fear came on all them that heard these things. And the young men arose, wound him up, and carried him out, and buried him. And it was about the space of three hours after, when his wife, not knowing what was done, came in. And Peter answered unto her, Tell me whether ye sold the land for so much? And she said, Yea, for so much. Then Peter said unto her, How is it that ye have agreed together to tempt the Spirit of the Lord? Behold, the feet of them which have buried thy husband are at the door, and shall carry thee out."

Acts 5:3-9

In the above story, Ananias and Sapphira were a married couple among the followers of Jesus. They agreed together with the other members of the Jerusalem church to sell some property and bring the money to the group for the mutual benefit of all of them. Unfortunately, after they had sold their land, the couple decided not to bring the whole amount to the group. They agreed as a couple to lie to the church. They eventually lost their lives.

Peter told them that Satan had filled their hearts to lie to the Holy Spirit. The question is: did they know that it was Satan that filled their hearts to lie? Also, what made it possible for Satan to fill their hearts? Furthermore, why should they be the only ones among the group that Satan was able to influence? And what would Satan gain by making them lie?

I believe this couple did not know that it was Satan using them. They thought they were acting alone. This couple probably lied so that they could use part of the money for personal needs. Their problem started at the time when they agreed with other members in the group to sell their property and bring in the money. They followed the crowd. They did not want other people to see them as different. They chose to follow the crowd, and made promises without proper consideration. They now faced anxiety when it was time to fulfil the promise. This anxiety is what opened the door to Satan to give them a suggestion.

Anxiety or fear is of the flesh, and whenever our flesh is allowed to take charge of our minds, Satan gains entrance. Satan probably had no definite target. Whoever among the group that fell into the same error as Ananias and Sapphira would have come under the same deception. Satan is naturally a destroyer and he rejoices when he is given the opportunity to destroy. Nobody is immune to the wiles of Satan. Whoever follows the flesh makes himself or herself a potential target of Satan.

You must be aware that you will open yourself up to satanic influence if you make a vow without proper consideration. Whenever you allow the flesh to dictate your decisions, you make yourself vulnerable to Satan's deception. Avoid putting yourself under pressure, because it makes you vulnerable and exposes you to Satan's manipulation. Decisions made under a cloud of uncertainty are an open door to satanic deception.

There are so many partners that make a vow to their spouse without proper consideration of the consequences, and when the time for fulfilling their promise comes they become anxious. This can open a door to Satan. He will start filling their hearts with a series of lies they could tell in order to escape their promise. If they give in to the temptation to lie, it is only a matter of time before their deception will be exposed. This may be the beginning of mistrust and the loss of integrity in a marriage.

7. SATAN IS A FOWLER

"Surely he shall deliver thee from the snare of the fowler, and from the noisome pestilence."

Psalm 91:3

A fowler is someone who hunts wild birds for food. He uses traps or snares to catch his prey. Satan is like an evil fowler, capturing his prey using many different traps. He can organise traps to destroy a home. Satan studies the victim he is targeting for years, and understands his weaknesses. He uses these to trap his prey.

What are your weaknesses? If your weakness is a fierce show of anger, Satan can trap you with it one day. Through anger, Satan has been able to lure people into action that results in death – both spiritual and physical.

Your weakness could be misuse of the tongue. Some people have cursed their partners with vicious words, enabling Satan to gain entrance into their marriage to start trouble. Your weakness could be that you are careless in your dealings with the opposite sex. Satan could use an attractive opposite sex friend to lure you into sexual sin. Some people have committed adultery or have been raped by an evil person by the use of 'date rape drugs'. The attacker puts a sleeping pill or incapacitating drug in the drink of their victim, and the person falls asleep or is rendered semi-conscious. While unconscious or vulnerable, the victim is manipulated into having sex with the attacker. Unfortunately, pregnancy can occur even with just one sexual encounter. This is a recipe for marriage destruction.

I pray that every trap Satan is organising against your marriage will fail, in Jesus' precious name.

8. SATAN IS A FOWL

"And when he sowed, some seeds fell by the way side, and the fowls came and devoured them up..."

Matthew 13:4

A fowl is a bird. Birds eat seeds that are exposed on the ground. Any seed that is not covered up is open to the attack of a bird. Satan is a thief and whatever is left unattended or unprotected can be stolen by him.

For example, you need to protect your home against financial crises, otherwise when you face a financial problem Satan could exploit it to break up your home. Many homes are destroyed these days because they have no proper financial protection – no savings or not enough insurance. So when a partner loses a job, or the house is burgled, or the couple gets into debt, the marriage is endangered.

You also need to protect your home against home wreckers. There are people who go around destroying homes through sexual seduction, gossiping, and every kind of malicious action. Protect your spouse, children and every good plan God has for your home.

May God surround your home with the walls of His fire, in the powerful name of Jesus.

8. SATAN IS A SOWER OF TARES

"But while men slept, his enemy came and sowed tares among the wheat, and went his way."

Matthew 13:25

Satan is a sower of tares. He is an expert in sowing weeds among the good crops. Tares will not let good crops grow. They kill crops through starving them of nutrition or sunlight. Tares compete with crops for food, water and space to grow.

THE ENEMY OF Marriage

There are things that will crowd out and starve the love in your relationship. Avoid them. Satan can sow incessant accusation, complaints, nagging, irritations, ignoring, finger-pointing, dissatisfaction, etc. Do not make yourself unpleasant to your spouse. This will not let love grow in your marriage.

Whatever hinders peaceful co-existence in your marriage is a tare and you must exclude it. When Satan puts a thought in your heart that would make you sow tares in your marriage, cast it out.

9. SATAN IS A WOLF

"But he that is an hireling, and not the shepherd, whose own the sheep are not, seeth the wolf coming, and leaveth the sheep, and fleeth: and the wolf catcheth them, and scattereth the sheep."

John 10:12

A wolf is an animal that attacks and scatters other animals weaker than itself, like sheep. Satan is a wolf. He is able to operate as a wolf through human vessels he uses. Satan may put the spirit of the wolf in the hearts of relatives and friends, leading them to attack and break up a home. Many homes have been destroyed by human wolves.

Be aware that there are people who Satan may raise up to destroy your relationship with your spouse. These are home destroyers. They come as friends and well-wishers, but soon they start turning the hearts of couples against each other. There are in-laws that have the wolf spirit inside them. They come to attack and scatter your family. They are the ones who always find fault in your dealings with your spouse. They may attack your way of doing things in your marital home. They may come as an accuser – always accusing you or your spouse of wrongdoing to one or the other. These are wolves seeking the destruction of your marriage.

When you notice such people around you, pray for wisdom in how to handle them and how to draw your spouse closer. Pray aggressively against the wolf spirit in your marriage, and very soon the attackers will be driven away by God.

I pray that every attacker hired against your marriage shall fail, in Jesus' wonderful name.

10. SATAN IS A ROARING LION

"Be sober, be vigilant; because your adversary the devil, as a roaring lion, walketh about, seeking whom he may devour."

1 Peter 5:8

To roar means to make a deep, prolonged, loud noise. Satan roars. He makes a loud noise to frighten people. The purpose of this is to make people scatter, creating confusion and panic. When people are in this kind of state they become vulnerable. They look for help, security or advice in the wrong places, and fall into a serious problem that may pave the way for Satan to swallow them. Satan knows that if people can be made confused and disoriented, they will become an easy prey to him.

When your marriage faces some challenges, be very careful how you handle the situation. Satan may start to roar. He may start exaggerating the situation and use your imagination against you. He will start attacking your mind with fear. He is roaring. The purpose is to lead you into error. Through error, Satan has been able to destroy so many people. Through error, Satan has been able to lure people into a practice that will bring destruction into their homes. Avoid emotional imbalance in all situations.

May God frustrate every attempt of Satan to lead you into error, in Jesus' glorious name.

11. Satan is a Serpent

"And the great dragon was cast out, that old serpent, called the Devil, and Satan, which deceiveth the whole world: he was cast out into the earth, and his angels were cast out with him."

Revelation 12:9

Satan is likened to a serpent. The serpent is crafty; he never walks straight. Satan is never straightforward. He walks in a zig-zag manner. He never shows the full picture of a thing. Avoid ideas that look good but are not clear. Avoid sweet thoughts of the mind that are without any clarity. Many homes have been destroyed because of plans that look good but are not godly.

Satan is a deceiver. A deceiver never shows the full picture. He will tell you the good side only, hiding the bad side. Do not be too quick to chase a dream or vision just because you think it will benefit your family. Get the full picture, praying that God should show you all the hidden details. Understand what you are going into and note that the consequence will not only affect you but the whole family. Satan is a deceiver, who always makes his plans appear good to his victims. He will hide the challenges and unforeseen costs.

Serpents have poison. Satan is poisonous and he is an expert in generating poison in a relationship. He knows how to make couples hate each other. Whenever you dwell on a negative situation in your marriage for a long time, Satan will use it to poison your heart. Concentrating on your spouse's careless words or actions will create bitterness of the heart that is potentially able to make you lose interest in the marriage. Do not dwell too long on an offence that happens between you and your spouse. Forgive and be reconciled as soon as possible. If you don't, Satan will use the situation to poison your mind towards your spouse.

This could be the beginning of lukewarmness towards each other in the relationship. It may make you see no future in the marriage.

Divorce could become an easy option. The genesis of it is a poison from Satan. Avoid storing negative things about your marriage in your heart. Do not be too easily offended by your spouse, otherwise your hearts may be poisoned towards each other. Bitterness of the heart is very difficult to cure once it takes root. Avoid it.

12. SATAN IS A REMOVER OF GOOD SEED

"When any one heareth the word of the kingdom, and understandeth it not, then cometh the wicked one, and catcheth away that which was sown in his heart. This is he which received seed by the way side."

Matthew 13:19

Every good seed that is not properly rooted will be taken away by Satan. If you forget your spouse's good words and treatment of you, they cannot take root in your heart and Satan will soon take them away. You must take to heart every good thing that has happened in your marriage. Offer thanks to God for it. Then it will always come into your remembrance whenever there is a challenge in your relationship.

There are many good memories you can keep. There are many good things that have taken place in your marriage. Dwell on them and let them take root in your heart. This will motivate you and enable you to dwell in the memory of good things.

When people only talk about the challenges their marriage is facing, the memory of good things that have happened will not come alive when they face contrary situations. Every good thing that has no deep root will be stolen by Satan. Focus on the good things and the good attributes of your spouse to motivate yourself. Do not live in the forgetfulness of good memory. Do not let Satan take away from your memory, the good things that have taken place in your marriage. Stop focusing on the bad side of your home.

13. SATAN IS A SIFTER

"And the Lord said, Simon, Simon, behold, Satan hath desired to have you, that he may sift you as wheat..."

Luke **22:31.**

Satan is a sifter. Sifting is done through agitation and violent shaking. Through sifting, certain things will be lost or not remembered. Satan loves to agitate the mind of people so that they forget all the good ideas in them and follow wrong paths that lead to destruction.

Through Satan's sifting, many people have behaved in an unwise manner. They were not able to put into practice all the good teaching and lessons of the past. Agitation of the mind makes an adult behave childishly. Avoid situations that will shake your resolve and faith. If you allow worry and anxiety to dominate your mind, you will lose your peace of heart. When this happens, you are likely to behave and plan in an unwise manner. This is because Satan has shifted from you all the good ideas and lessons life has taught you for a day like this. Trials of life open the door to Satan to sift a man. He exploits challenges to agitate the mind.

I pray that any situation the enemy wants to exploit to agitate your mind will fail, in Jesus' name.

14. SATAN IS A WASTER

"Behold, I have created the smith that bloweth the coals in the fire, and that bringeth forth an instrument for his work; and I have created the waster to destroy."

Isaiah 54:16

Satan is a waster. He devours and ruins. He knows how to influence a person to waste their life. He can make someone do nothing good with all the opportunities around him.

God has brought you into marriage with your spouse, and He is busy creating many opportunities for you to have a better life together. Therefore, Satan will attempt to keep both of you busy with irrelevant things, or create strife between you, so that you will be blind to all the blessings God is sending to you.

Satan the waster makes people waste opportunities by causing distractions around them. Similarly, Satan can deflect the destiny of people by making them work against the purpose of God for their lives.

Satan is making so many children become wasters themselves. Such children benefit nobody. They are useless, despite the fact that God loves them and has good plans and purposes for them.

There are so many couples wasting away. They are more interested pointing out each other's flaws and mistakes than in fulfilling God's purpose. Do not waste your time, talents and money, and do not allow Satan to influence your home to waste away. There is a good reason why you have married the person you married. If you are both Christians, you are together for a purpose. If you fail to fulfil this purpose, your marital life is a waste of a God-given opportunity. May God make you wiser than your enemy, by the power of Jesus' name.

15. SATAN IS AN INTRUDER

"Now the serpent was more subtil than any beast of the field which the LORD God had made. And he said unto the woman, Yea, hath God said, Ye shall not eat of every tree of the garden?"

Genesis 3:1

In this verse, Satan was not invited into the affairs of the family of Adam and Eve. He just came into their home and started a discussion. An intruder is a person who enters into a place without invitation. You do not need to invite Satan into the affairs of your home; he will definitely come whenever he sees an open door to enter. Satan monitors and closely observes events going on around you. Whenever he sees an opportunity to intrude into the affairs of a home, he dives in. That is why you must not open a door for Satan to intrude into your marriage. Every ungodliness is an open door to Satan to come in and work against your relationship. Be wise.

While men slept

"But while men slept, his enemy came and sowed tares among the wheat, and went his way."

Matthew 13:25

The most likely time for Satan to strike is while you are sleeping – in other words, when you are not alert. It is very unlikely that you will intentionally agree or work with Satan to destroy your marriage. It has to happen without your consciousness or awareness.

The times you are 'asleep' include the following:

1. WHEN YOU HARDEN YOUR HEART

"While it is said, today if ye will hear his voice, harden not your hearts, as in the provocation."

Hebrews 3:15

This is the time when you refuse to repent of certain wrong actions or deeds. When you harden your heart, you open a door to Satan to lure you into more sin. This period is considered as the time you 'sleep' because you are acting blindly, without seeing what is awaiting you. Avoid hardness of heart. Be quick to accept apologies from your spouse. Be quick to practise forgiveness. Be quick to repent of all wrongdoings. The more you delay, the more difficult it becomes to do.

2. WHEN YOU CHOOSE TO WALK IN SELF-DECEPTION

"For if a man think himself to be something, when he is nothing, he deceiveth himself."

Galatians 6:3

This is the time when you have every opportunity to make the right decision but you choose to go your own way. You start deceiving yourself that you can handle all situations. You choose to follow the wrong path, knowingly, but without a full understanding of the consequences of your action. You boast that you can handle anything, forgetting that you have limited abilities. But, you will soon cry out when you face a situation that is too big for you to handle. You have been sleeping in the spirit. You chose to walk in self-deception.

You are a human being with limited capability. Do not see yourself as more than what you actually are. We all need to depend on God. Self-deception makes it easy for Satan to use you for his evil mission. Know your strength. Know that if you did not need a spouse, God would not have given you one. If you could live alone without any helper, God would not have allowed you to marry. Stop thinking you are more than your real self. Stop telling yourself that you can live a better life without your spouse. You need each other, both for now and the days ahead.

3. WHEN YOU ALLOW EMOTION TO TAKE OVER YOUR REASONING

Emotion is a mental state that arises spontaneously rather than through conscious effort. It's about how you feel. Your emotions can rise up when you are in situations that cause joy, sorrow, reverence, hate, love, etc.

Usually, after some time, your emotional state returns to normal. But while active, emotions make people act, talk and vow in a way they would not have done naturally. When the emotion wears off or dies down, they start regretting their actions and words. They have been 'sleeping' unknowingly. They have allowed emotion to take over their reasoning and consciousness. Be aware that people who are unable to control their emotions are easy prey to Satan.

"But when Herod's birthday was kept, the daughter of Herodias danced before them, and pleased Herod. Whereupon he promised with an oath to give her whatsoever she would ask. And she, being before instructed of her mother, said, give me here John Baptist's head in a charger. And the king was sorry: nevertheless for the oath's sake, and them which sat with him at meat, he commanded it to be given her."

Matthew 14:6-9

In this story, King Herod made a vow out of emotion and later regretted it. By the time he realised his error, it was too late to change it. Emotion will allow Satan to use you against your marriage. For example, the emotion of anger can open the door to satanic invasion. Many people have destroyed their marriage due to their hot temper. You must stay in control.

4. WHEN YOU ACT UNDER TIREDNESS

When you are physically, mentally or emotionally tired, you are open to Satan's attack. During this time, you are not in total control of yourself. Also, your senses are not all that active, so you are more vulnerable and may be 'asleep' to the tactics of the enemy.

If you enter into any form of negotiation at such times, Satan will take advantage of your tiredness and try to lure you into error. In *Genesis 25:30-34*, Esau negotiated with Jacob when he was "faint" (verse 30). He sold his birth-right. According to *Hebrews 12:17*, Esau attempted to change the transaction after he regained his strength, but it was too late. He entered into negotiation when his mental faculties were dulled by tiredness.

Many married people have lost their partner or damaged their relationship because they took an irreversible decision during their time of tiredness. Satan took advantage of their weakness and spoiled their precious marriage.

5. WHEN YOU STAY IN THE WRONG PLACE AT THE WRONG TIME

You are vulnerable to Satan's attack when you stay in a wrong place at a wrong time. You can expose yourself to temptation that may be beyond your spiritual resistance. In a wrong place, your spiritual alertness will not be active.

"And it came to pass, after the year was expired, at the time when kings go forth to battle, that David sent Joab, and his servants with him, and all Israel; and they destroyed the children of Ammon, and besieged Rabbah. But David tarried still at Jerusalem. And it came to pass in an eveningtide, that David arose from off his bed, and walked upon the roof of the king's house: and from the roof he saw a woman washing herself; and the woman was very beautiful to look upon."

2 Samuel 11:1-2

In this story, David should have been away fighting the Lord's battles, instead of which he stayed behind in Jerusalem, and exposed his heart to temptation. He chose to stay in the wrong place at the wrong time. This bad decision lured David into adultery and murder. He brought avoidable danger upon his family. His spiritual antennae could not pick up the danger. David's spiritual sensitivity was totally paralysed. His conscience could not wake him up from the slumber.

The situation was so bad that David only realised his error when the Prophet Nathan came to rebuke him, as recorded in 2Samuel

12. As a married person, there are certain gatherings you are not supposed to attend and certain places you should not be found. This is because you will expose yourself to temptation that may bring destruction upon your marriage. You will expose yourself to satanic manipulation when you stay in his territory.

6. WHEN YOU ENTER INTO AN EVIL ASSOCIATION

Satan dwells among evil people. Whenever such people gather, Satan is in their midst. You are risking your destruction if you get involved in evil associations. Among evil companions, your spiritual sensitivity will be reduced or ineffective. You will enter into a state of spiritual slumber.

In *Judges 16:4-30*, Samson began a relationship with a prostitute called Delilah. He allowed himself to live in a negative spiritual atmosphere. Delilah put pressure on him to reveal the secret of his power. Three times Delilah demanded to know the secret of his power. Samson never picked up that Delilah was up to something mischievous. He was in a deep spiritual slumber. The environment he was in paralysed his spiritual sensitivity.

Samson eventually died in the territory of his enemies. Evil associations will deactivate your spiritual sensitivity and you will expose yourself to satanic manipulation. People have destroyed their marriage through wrong relationships. Many married people have abandoned their partners due to the evil influence of wrong companions. Be careful about the people you associate with, otherwise, they may become an open door to satanic influence over you.

7. WHEN YOU OPEN UP YOUR SPIRIT TO DECEPTION

There are certain deceptive spiritual teachings that you should not allow entrance into your life. This is because when such destructive information enters your thoughts, you may allow it to take root in your spirit, and if you do it, the truth in you will be contaminated. Unknowingly, you will start behaving strangely, in accordance with the heresies you have allowed into yourself. That is why you need to be sure of your spiritual maturity before you listen to or study certain subjects.

When lies take root inside someone, they supress and annihilate the truth in you. You will then start acting out of that deception. You will go into a state of spiritual slumber, where you will not be able to discern between the truth and a lie.

"As we said before, so say I now again, if any man preach any other gospel unto you than that ye have received, let him be accursed."

Galatians 1:9

This Bible verse says that you should avoid being persuaded or taken in by any message that contradicts the Bible. The Bible contains all the information you need for salvation – and for a successful marriage. Marriage was established by God and not man. The secret of successful marriage is in the hand of God, who established it. Any teaching that is contrary to the Bible should not be given any attention. You must rebuke such counsel from the outset.

"And that because of false brethren unawares brought in, who came in privily to spy out our liberty which we have in Christ Jesus, that they might bring us into bondage…"

Galatians 2:4

This verse shows that heresies are designed to take away the liberty God has given us through Jesus Christ. Do not entertain wrong teaching. If you continually listen to and absorb contradictory information, sooner or later it will take root in your heart and you will start behaving in accordance with it. Satan introduces heresies in order to use them as avenues to catch people and lure them into wrong practices and beliefs. Do not open up your spirit to deception. The situation could go beyond your ability to manage.

8. WHEN YOU ACT FROM THE WRONG MOTIVE

Wrong motives will make you behave wrongly without knowing it. A bad motive exposes you to satanic manipulation. Whenever your motive for an action is wrong, you unwittingly come under the dictate of Satan. You enter into a state of spiritual sleep.

"Then said Jesus, Father, forgive them; for they know not what they do. And they parted his raiment, and cast lots."

Luke 23:34

Jesus prayed for those responsible for His persecution. He said they did not know what they were doing. The question is: Did they know that they did not know what they were doing? The answer is obvious. They did not know. But why? This is because their motive was wrong. They persecuted Jesus not because they loved God but because they were full of jealousy, as it says in Matthew 27:18: "For he knew that for envy they had delivered him."

The driving force behind their action was envy. This is what opened the door to Satan to use them. When Satan gains control of a person, such a person will no longer be able to control his action in totality. He will enter into a state of spiritual slumber.

If your motive of chasing a dream is to prove to your spouse that you are better than him or her, then you will open the door to Satan to gain control of you. From the point when Satan gains control of you, you will no longer be in full control of your actions. You no longer know what you are doing.

If you fail to quickly address your error (by repenting of your wrong motive), Satan will lure you to commit more error that is more capable of destroying your home. Always check your motive for every action you want to take. If it is wrong, you will expose yourself to satanic influence, unless you quickly repent.

Lest he takes advantage of us

"Lest Satan should get an advantage of us: for we are not ignorant of his devices."

2 Corinthians 2:11

Satan operates through issues. He takes advantage of the prevailing circumstances to operate in a relationship.

For example, people don't just fight unless something happens. Couples will not just wake up one day and decide to separate unless something happens between them. Some catalyst is needed for a couple to fight and separate.

Satan is always on the alert, monitoring a series of issues going on in a relationship. Whenever he notices that a couple are engaging in a hot argument or are dwelling on certain issues for a long time, he exploits the situation to fuel the crisis and expands it. If he is allowed, he can drag the matter to a level where the couple will foolishly agree to separate.

The reason why a couple may not see Satan at work in their relationship is because the issue they are fighting over actually exists. They see that as the problem, not the manipulator behind it. The couple unwittingly make each other a focus and start pointing accusing fingers at each other, criticising each other's actions and words.

This actually happens. It may be true that both the husband and wife have done certain wrong things and uttered certain wrong words. We are not ignoring the reality of what has happened. But what we know is that when Satan gets involved in the matter, the situation becomes unmanageable for the couple. They will forget that they once called each other nice names and had a good relationship together in the past.

Satan operates through issues. He exploits the prevailing circumstances in the marriage to drag the partners into the waters of strife and turn them against each other. That is why you must know that it is not about what happens in a relationship that matters most, but how we handle what happens. It is the way we respond to issues in our relationship that reveals our true nature, and will decide whether Satan becomes victorious in our lives or not.

"Woe unto the world because of offences! For it must needs be that offences come; but woe to that man by whom the offence cometh!"

Matthew 18:7

This verse shows the reality of offences. It shows that there will always be issues in a relationship. But we may begin to suspect that Satan is getting involved in the matter when the offence begins to control the people involved, and the situation becomes unmanageable. That is why you must be quick to forgive and quick to repent. When you practise quick forgiveness and repentance, you will be able to keep Satan out of your marital issues.

Satan will only gain entrance into the affairs of your home if you dwell on a negative situation for a long time. The longer you argue over an issue, or harbour it in your heart, the easier it is for Satan to manipulate your mind and thoughts. Once Satan is able to manipulate your mind, he will start planting actions and reactions into your mind that will complicate the matter. He will make you more and more bitter towards your spouse, deceiving you into making the wrong your spouse has done your complete focus.

When this happens, you begin to justify yourself for whatever steps you choose to take. Satan is at work at this stage. He is dragging you deeper into error, and can make you destroy your marriage by your self-justification.

Sin

Sin opens the door to satanic invasion.

"Hereafter I will not talk much with you: for the prince of this world cometh, and hath nothing in me."

John 14:30

Sin is Satan's tool. Wherever sin exists, Satan gains entrance. If you do not want Satan to use you to destroy your marriage, you must keep holy. Sin will take away your resistance to satanic influence. It will make you an easy target for him.

You need to understand the full meaning of sin. Sin is the nature of a man that opposes everything that is good and of God. Sin is not limited to obvious immoral acts like adultery, murder, lying, violence or stealing. Sin also includes abuse of the mind.

You are abusing your mind whenever you engage it in unholy thoughts. Such abuses of the mind include anxiety, fear, worry, anger, bitterness, pride, jealousy, doubt, etc. All these could be classified as mental sins. Whenever you engage your mind in such negative thoughts, you open the way for Satan to tempt you into a wrong action, decision or words. Wrong words are verbal sins, which originate from speaking words that don't glorify the name of God. Such words include abusiveness, lying, gossiping, cursing, etc.

The battle against things of the flesh will be fought throughout our entire lifetime.

"For the flesh lusteth against the Spirit, and the Spirit against the flesh: and these are contrary the one to the other: so that ye cannot do the things that ye would."

Galatians 5:17

This verse is applicable to every human being, irrespective of the level of their spirituality. There is a constant war going on between the flesh and the spirit. Satan works in collaboration with the flesh and this is what enables him to gain entrance into the affairs of a home. This implies that the more you are able to rule over the flesh, the more you will be able to prevent Satan from interfering in your marriage.

Similarly, the more you are able to identify when your spouse is under satanic influence, the more you will be able to hinder Satan from using your spouse to destroy your marriage. Even when it is impossible for you to stop your spouse from allowing Satan to use him/her, your spiritual sensitivity will enable you to avoid what Satan wants to do through your spouse. When your spouse becomes irrational, your sensitivity will tell you that Satan is at work. Therefore you should control your own emotional response, and seek the face of God for divine intervention.

The fabric of the home

A home has structure. There are different ligaments that join together to form a home. Satan targets each ligament and attempts to destroy it. When he succeeds in destroying these ligaments, the marriage collapses – like a house with broken walls.

The structure of a godly home has different ligaments such as: prayer, faith, obedience, unity, peace, respect, sound-mind, health, finance, communication, and children. These are things that keep a home together and enable it to function appropriately. In the next chapters, you will discover how Satan attacks different ligaments of the structure of a home. You will also discover the kind of doctrines Satan has released into the world today in order to destroy marriage.

Prayer

Any door either myself or my partner may have created for satanic operation in our home, be closed now, in Jesus' name.

Any lion roaring against peace and prosperity in my home – the Lord rebuke you in Jesus' name.

In the name of Jesus, Father, overthrow any host of wickedness on assignment against my home.

I command any sword the enemy raises against my marriage to turn against the enemy, in Jesus' name.

I command all the troublers of my marriage to be scattered by fire of the Lord, in Jesus' name.

Power or spirit or personality assigned from hell to trick me or my partner out of our marriage, fall and die in Jesus' name.

Spirit of deception that turns partners against each other, you shall not prosper in my home, in Jesus' name.

Wherever carnality is reigning in any affair of my home, I dethrone you now, in Jesus' name.

Power of offence, strife, accusation and counter-accusation, fail in my home, in Jesus' name.

Any blessing the enemy has stolen from my home, I recover it now with dividend – in Jesus' name.

3
The Power of Knowledge

"And the LORD God commanded the man, saying, of every tree of the garden thou mayest freely eat: But of the tree of the knowledge of good and evil, thou shalt not eat of it: for in the day that thou eatest thereof thou shalt surely die."

Genesis 2:16-17

Knowledge is the possession of information, or perception of the truth about a situation. It is correct information you perceive, discover, learn or are told about.

In *Genesis 2:16-17*, God did not want man to have the knowledge of good and evil in this world. This is because what man knows will control him, and God wanted to be the only one who controls man. Therefore, God wanted man to know only those things that He would show to him. Unfortunately, man went ahead and ate the forbidden fruit. Man now knows a lot, but to his own detriment.

James 3:15-17 shows that there are two types of wisdom. This implies that there are also two types of knowledge. There is evil knowledge and there is good knowledge. Good knowledge leads a man to God, while evil knowledge leads a man away from God. Even in your marriage, if you can gain more good knowledge about your spouse and ignore the evil knowledge that Satan is giving you concerning your spouse, you will create more bonds between yourself and your spouse.

All the bad things you have stored in your mind towards your spouse are as a result of the fallen nature of man. In the beginning, before the fall of man in the Garden of Eden, the first couple had no evil knowledge about each other. For example, Adam and Eve never accused each other until sin crept into their relationship through Satan's deception.

The fallen nature of man has led him into more discoveries that unfortunately are dragging him away from God.

"But thou, O Daniel, shut up the words, and seal the book, even to the time of the end: many shall run to and fro, and knowledge shall be increased."

Daniel 12:4

Indeed, knowledge has increased. Man always seeks for more knowledge. Unfortunately, man knows more about evil than he knows about good. That's simply because he is fallen and therefore more attracted by evil. He desires to know more about the negative knowledge than that which is positive.

This is the reason why Satan is bombarding you with more negative knowledge about your spouse. Satan cleverly leads you to discover negative things about your spouse to counteract the positive things you have discovered. This is because Satan knows that what a man knows will control him. The more bad things you know about your spouse, the worse you will behave towards him/her. All the accusations you direct at your spouse result from the negative things you know about him/her. That is why if you want your marriage to succeed, you must stop finding fault with your spouse and concentrate on his/her good points.

The consequences of negative knowledge in marriage include the following:

1. Seeing Evil in Each Other Continually

Many homes are in conflict because the two partners always see evil in each other. Before the fall of man, Adam and Eve never saw evil in each other – because it wasn't there! But after the fall, there was evil to notice. In *Genesis 3*, Adam told God that it was the wife He gave him that caused Adam's disobedience. He saw evil in Eve, and used it as an excuse for his own evil.

Most of the crises in marriages today can be linked to the fact that the partners always see evil in each other. They are continually finding fault in each other. If you want to build a glorious home, you need to stop finding fault in your spouse. Marriage is not about who is better, but the grace of God. Incessant criticism of your spouse will open the door to Satan to use your evil knowledge about your spouse. He will use it to destroy your home. Be warned. Always focus on the strengths, not the weaknesses. Weaknesses should be prayed for, not used as a weapon against your spouse.

May God anoint your eye to see as God wants you to see, in Jesus' name.

2. Evil Imagination and Expectations

Due to what man knows about good and evil, man faces life imagining evil where it does not exist and expecting others to behave in evil ways.

Today people argue over such trivial things. Many couples fight over what isn't even real – they just imagine it. Others don't even wait for their spouses to divorce before they initiate it, because they imagine the worst about their spouse and believe it. Some people imagine that very soon their homes will break up. Some people have such a negative view of life that they believe a certain evil will happen, and then it does happen because Satan manipulates their negativity.

In *Genesis 12:11-13*, Abraham just imagined that the Egyptians would kill him in order to take his wife, Sarah. Based on this negative imagination, he persuaded Sarah to agree to lie and say she was his sister. As a result, Abraham lost his wife to Pharaoh, and later the lie was exposed and Abraham and Sarah were thrown out of Egypt.

If you want your home to stand, you will need to stop imagining evil. May God wash your mind clean, in Jesus' name.

3. Loss of Liberty

Evil knowledge steals liberty and choice. It makes it difficult for couples to explore certain new opportunities in their lives together, because they think that their partner's weaknesses may undermine their plans. Many people no longer walk in freedom because of what they know to be evil.

In many homes, it is difficult for couples to work together because they know a lot of negative things about each other. They can't relate freely to each other or exercise trust due to negative things they have stored in their minds towards each other. It is better to take negative things you know about your spouse to God in prayer, instead of allowing that knowledge to take away your marital freedom.

4. Hopelessness

Due to what they know about each other, some couples consider certain situations in their home to be hopeless. For example, some people believe that their spouses will never change due to negative knowledge they have about their spouse's stubborn nature.

When certain things happen in some families, the couple will say it is a hopeless case and that there is no solution. They are talking from what they know about knowledge of this world and human nature, and not the knowledge of God that has no limitation.

In *Mark 5:35-43*, the daughter of Jairus was sick and later he was told that she had died. When Jesus came to the house, He said the girl was not dead but asleep. The crowd laughed at Him because of their knowledge of what it means to die. They exalted what they knew about death above what they knew about God. Many couples have lost miracles and divine intervention due to their knowledge about illnesses.

May your knowledge never rob you of the faith for miracles, in Jesus' name.

5. EVIL CONFESSION

There are many homes engulfed in evil confessions. As a result, such homes swim in a river of continual affliction.

If you fail to control the knowledge you have about certain events, you will be speaking into your situation based on such knowledge and not from what God says concerning it.

Many couples live in sorrow because of what an expert told them about their situation. They confess impossibility, just as they were told by the so-called experts. You may need to start confessing what God says concerning your marriage and stop speaking negative reports of men. Non-Christian experts may be right about what nature does on its own, but they have no understanding of what God can do.

If you refuse to switch from what you know to what God has taught you, you will soon develop a habit of evil confession which will attract more evil into your life and marriage.

For example, in *Exodus 14*, Israel said they would die when they saw Pharaoh chasing them. They knew that Pharaoh was a murderer, so they spoke from what they knew. But they forgot that God had promised them life through the demonstration of His power in many situations of their lives. Unfortunately, this lack of faith became their habit and usual manner of response to every difficult situation. They eventually died in the desert instead of the Promised Land, as recorded in Numbers 14, due to their evil confessions.

I pray that every item of knowledge that you have that attracts evil into your life, will be wiped from your memory today, in Jesus' name.

6. Deception

The prince of this world is Satan and he is the one who defines what is good and evil in the eyes of this world. What Satan calls good, is designed to lure man into sin.

Today, many people unknowingly have fellowship with the devil. He speaks deceptive words into the minds of people, which they use to operate their lives. Man no longer defines good and evil according to the knowledge of God, but according to their own thinking – which comes from Satan.

It is a deception for you to think that you can change your spouse through the use of force. It is a deception for you to try to do what only God can do. It is a deception for you to expect from man what only God can do for you. Your spouse is not God; he/she has limited ability. Do not expect from man what only God can do in your life.

Expecting too much of your spouse, believing that he/she can fulfil all your needs, can only come from Satan and not God. It is a deception. It is not realistic. Such expectations will breed unreasonable disappointment in you, because what you are asking of your spouse is something that can only be given by God. You need to stop focusing on your spouse to supply all your needs, because that will breed frustration, which will deceive you into bad practices which may destroy your marriage.

Similarly, stop trying to do in your marriage what only God can do. If you have failed to implement certain changes in your marriage, do not be too quick to blame yourself or your spouse for such failure. It maybe because you are attempting to do what only God can do for you.

I pray that any veil of deception operating in your life shall be destroyed today by the fire of God, in Jesus' name.

7. RESTLESSNESS

If good or evil is defined in a way that is contrary to God's revelation, it will lead to a restless life. Satan is the father of all wanderers and through his evil knowledge is able to make people live a life of fear and restlessness.

Many people see fear where there is no fear. This is because of what they claim to know. Knowledge from Satan takes away peace. You must learn how to explain and define situations of your marriage in accordance with the Word of God, so that you do not unwittingly use the descriptions and explanations of Satan to interpret your marital issues.

In 1 Samuel 1, the Bible says that God closed the womb of Hannah and that is why she was barren for some time. But the culture of her land said that barrenness was the result of a curse. This is a contradiction of what the Bible says. A couple who believe what their culture says will be running here and there, looking for solutions all over the place, instead of waiting for God to open what He has closed. Define and explain the situations in your marriage according to biblical teaching and not according to what the world has taught you.

I pray that the power of God will today take you out of every race you are running that God has not given you, in Jesus' name.

What fuels this knowledge?

There are certain factors around us and in us as human beings that will open doors to Satan, luring us into embracing evil knowledge. You need to identify these factors and bring them under control through the power of the Holy Spirit, so that they cannot be exploited by Satan to manipulate your knowledge.

1. THE FALLEN NATURE OF MAN

Man naturally thinks evil things due to his fallen nature.

"And God saw that the wickedness of man was great in the earth, and that every imagination of the thoughts of his heart was only evil continually."

Genesis 6:5

It has become the nature of man to think evil. The natural man doesn't need training to think or do evil. It is his nature. For example, nobody trained Cain how to be bitter and how to kill. He killed Abel in Genesis4. It is in the fallen nature of man. This makes it easy for Satan to manipulate man to decide what is good or bad in accordance to his dictate.

In order to avoid the error of ruling your life with evil knowledge, you will need to constantly bring yourself under the control of the Holy Spirit. Allow the Holy Spirit to minister into your spirit in all situations. Thoughts and imaginations that do not agree with the Word of God should not be entertained.

"For if ye live after the flesh, ye shall die: but if ye through the Spirit do mortify the deeds of the body, ye shall live."

Romans 8:13

You will need to put your flesh – your sinful nature – under God's control, because Satan communicates to man through his flesh. The fallen nature in you will become more and more ineffective as you crucify the flesh more and more.

I pray that every remaining work of the flesh in you shall be burnt away by the fire of God today, in Jesus' name.

2. SOCIETY AROUND US

Satan is the prince of this world and he is continually feeding society with his ideas and counsel. He saturates society with an incessant flow of negative thoughts and bad news. This is to ensure that man continually thinks, imagines and confesses such news.

For example, media houses continually feed the world with a flow of negative reports which are broadcast in the news. This opens the door to Satan to gain control of the minds of those who listen to such news, and influences them to think and imagine evil.

In Numbers 13, those who went to spy on the land brought back a negative report which spread round the camp and nearly all those who heard it believed. Today, people find it easier to believe bad news than good. It is because their minds have been trained to think so through their constant exposure to bad news.

As a married person, you must separate yourself from the world and control your exposure to information from the world. Do not send into your spirit, every piece of news from the world, for this will influence your thinking pattern.

There are so many negative news stories about marriage coming into your home through different sources. Such news and reports make marriage seem impracticable and impossible. They paint marriage as a union that can't be maintained in today's civilisation. This makes some people and society in general describe marriage in the context of their weak and poor moral values. As a married person, do not fill your spirit with such negative advertisements about marriage because, if you do, it will make you negative towards your spouse. You may also fall into the deception of evil expectations about your marriage, seeing it as an institution that will soon fail in your life.

I pray that every evil reporter hired against you shall fail in his mission, in Jesus' name.

3. Past experience

What has happened to man makes a stain on his memory. If not properly guided, past events in your marriage may influence you to think negatively towards your spouse and your marriage.

Past failure and disappointment from your spouse may make you think negatively towards him/her whenever there is an issue that requires trust between you. Do not allow past disappointment from your spouse to make you believe that there will never be a change. Your spouse can change, and you must relate with him/her in faith that change is possible. Do not turn yourself into a prophet of doom over your marriage, based on past events. Stop forecasting failure and mistrust concerning your marriage. Do not let Satan exploit your past experience to determine your thinking pattern towards your spouse.

I pray that every kind of knowledge in you that will not let you obey the voice of God shall be wiped from your memory today, in Jesus' name.

4. Your belief system

Your beliefs can open a door to Satan to make you think and walk in evil knowledge. You will see the situation according to what you believe.

If you believe in love, you will always see good in your spouse. This makes you a friendly spouse to him/her. Conversely, if you believe in hatred, you will always see offence in your spouse. This will make you always try to avoid him/her. Also, if you believe in failure, you will always know a lot about failure and how to justify it. This can even make you believe that your marriage may fail at any time. But if you believe in success, you will always see success and possibility in your marriage.

You will relate to your spouse according to your beliefs.

"We having the same spirit of faith, according as it is written, I believed, and therefore have I spoken; we also believe, and therefore speak..."

2 Corinthians 4:13

Believe in trust, not mistrust. Believe in unity, not disunity. Believe in love, not hatred. In all that concerns your marriage, let faith guide you, not past negative experience.

It is my prayer that God will overhaul your belief system for His own glory, in Jesus' name.

5. HOPE DEFERRED

A problem that refuses to be solved impacts on people, making them think negatively about the future. This could invite hopelessness. You must not allow a delay to your prayers or expectations to affect your relationship with your spouse. Do not associate such situations with your spouse's past errors. Refuse to agree with Satan that your present delay is your spouse's fault. Take every delay to God in prayer instead of speculating on who is to blame for it.

"Hope deferred maketh the heart sick: but when the desire cometh, it is a tree of life."

Proverbs 13:12.

I pray that every ungodly delay in your life shall receive the attention of God today, in Jesus' name.

Handling negative knowledge.

You must learn to handle whatever destructive knowledge the world is throwing at you, so that it doesn't damage your marriage. Effectively apply the following to all information you receive, before using that information in your marriage:

1. MAKE IT COMPLY WITH THE BIBLE

Whatever you know, either through the world's systems or your spouse's behaviour, make it comply with the Word of God. If it disagrees with the Word of God, discard it. It must promote the following three values: righteousness, peace and joy.

"For the kingdom of God is not meat and drink; but righteousness, and peace, and joy in the Holy Ghost."

Romans 14:17

Every piece of knowledge you possess about marriage must promote these three values. All the information about your spouse that you accept must promote these three values. If not, then separate yourself from them and never apply them to your relationship with your spouse.

2. IT MUST PASS THE TEST

You must test every idea or thought before you store it into your mind and spirit. Ensure that such knowledge passes the following test before you allow it to make an imprint in your spirit. Here's the test:

"Finally, brethren, whatsoever things are true, whatsoever things are honest, whatsoever things are just, whatsoever things are pure, whatsoever things are

lovely, whatsoever things are of good report; if there be any virtue, and if there be any praise, think on these things."

Philippians 4:8

Whatever you know about marriage and your spouse must be true (according to the Word of God), honest (no deception), just (promote righteousness and fair treatment), pure (have no sin), lovely (be friendly and attractive to good people), of good report (well-spoken and reputable in the kingdom of God), virtuous (excellent values) and praiseworthy (commendable by God and making God proud of you).

3. RENEW YOUR MIND

You may have been taught many things about marriage, and many of them may be wrong – judging by the standards of the kingdom of God. You will need to unlearn some of the things you have learned about marriage. You will need to get the junk out of your mind concerning marriage. Everything you think you know about marriage that is contrary to the Word of God must be thrown out of your mind.

You have to use the Word of God to renew your mind. Overhaul your beliefs and thinking system.

"And be not conformed to this world: but be ye transformed by the renewing of your mind, that ye may prove what is that good, and acceptable, and perfect, will of God."

Romans 12:2

This verse indicates that what is good is defined according to the definition of God – not of man.

Renewal of your mind will enable you to face the future with a pure heart, uncontaminated by the negative occurrences of the past and wrong information or teaching. Replace every single concept about marriage with what the Word of God says about it.

4. Exalt the Word of God

That is, let the Word of God come first in all your decisions. Always give the Word of God top priority.

"Casting down imaginations, and every high thing that exalteth itself against the knowledge of God, and bringing into captivity every thought to the obedience of Christ."

2 Corinthians 10:5

Exalt the Word of God above every policy, principle, knowledge, invention and philosophy of the world about marriage.

5. Live a life of faith

You can only please God by faith. You can't please God by what you know or don't know. But whatever prevents you from acting and living by faith doesn't please God. Any knowledge in you that will produce negative action and unbelief can never please God. You will need to quickly get rid of knowledge that makes you act like an unbeliever.

In *Luke 1:5-7*, Zacharias and Elisabeth were barren for some years, but they stayed together. The knowledge they held about marriage kept them together. Though, they were unable to have children for a long time, they did not die barren.

Faith will always please God and it will attract His action and involvement in a situation, so live a life of faith. Believe that change is possible. Don't take negative action in a negative situation. Trust God to bring change in His own time. Wait for divine intervention in all matters concerning your marriage. Situations can change.

Your spouse can also change in the way you desire, but it will happen at God's chosen time, not yours.

Their eyes were opened

"And the eyes of them both were opened, and they knew that they were naked; and they sewed fig leaves together, and made themselves aprons."

Genesis 3:7

After the fall of man, the man and woman's eyes were opened. This implies they now knew more than they knew before the fall. Indirectly, they became more civilised (starting to wear clothes). Unfortunately, it was to their detriment. They had acquired knowledge that they would not be able to handle.

We live in a world of intellectual knowledge. Man has so much knowledge that he thinks he has replaced God. But it is only the knowledge of God that will enable you to tame the knowledge of this world. That is why it is important for you to know more and more of God.

If you have learned things of this world at the expense of knowing about God, it will have a negative impact on you. It is not evil to increase in knowledge about the world, but you must not just increase in this world's knowledge without learning more of God's wisdom. This so-called civilised world has brought a great deal of destructive knowledge to marriage that you need to be aware of, so that it will not gain control of you and destroy your marriage.

1. HUMAN KNOWLEDGE WIDENS THE GAP BETWEEN MAN AND GOD

In *Genesis 3:24* after the fall, the first couple were expelled from the presence of God. Since then, knowledge outside of God always widens the gap between man and God. Whatever you think you

THE ENEMY OF Marriage

know about marriage that conflicts with the Bible will create a gap between you and God as regards the marriage.

Due to this gap, many Christians use the world's systems to handle marital issues, instead of the Bible. Even their counsellors may not be godly but from the world. Their marriage counsellors have often been divorced themselves, indicating that the counsel they use to help others failed in their own lives and isn't trustworthy.

2. IT BREEDS CONFUSION

Many marriages have been destroyed today because of the struggle to fit into the world of sophistication we live in. People's opinions, views and even tastes keep on changing, as more discoveries are made or research is done. What you were told was a good idea one day, is no longer a good idea the next. You will need to bring your personal preferences under the control of the Holy Spirit, otherwise they may lead you into evil. Due to pressures and stress, many homes have been destroyed by Satan. Control your ambition. Control what you are chasing.

3. IT CREATES SELF-RELIANCE

The knowledge of this world has advanced and there are more discoveries every day. We now have more facilities that can make our lives more comfortable.

Unfortunately, many people are deceived to believe that they can substitute their spouse with what the world can provide for them. Some people believe that they don't need to marry. They are taught that the world has alternatives for them that are better than marriage. They are told to rely on themselves, and that marriage will make them rely on another person. This is a lie. Marriage creates a helper and companion. It is a good plan of God that a man and a woman live together as married people. Do not treat your spouse as a non-essential factor in your life. You will always need a helper in the journey of life.

4. It causes perversion

Today marriage principles are perverted because people become more and more irresponsible. In order to avoid responsibility, they create a means of easy escape from marriage.

The world has also come up with alternatives to male-female marriage. These include gay marriage, lesbianism, masturbation, sleeping around, etc. All these are perversions of God's plan and you should not see them as a way of escape from marriage. You must appreciate your spouse as an opposite sex to yourself. You must appreciate the differences between the two of you. Avoid any form of perversion. Do not see masturbation as an alternative to sex. Perversion invites demons into marriage.

5. It causes inequality

Men do not all advance at the same rate in knowledge. The world we live in is full of inequality. Inequality makes people feel cheated. Husbands and wives do not have the same treatment under the law in many countries today. That is why the Bible must be the final authority in the affairs of your home. In certain societies, the law seems to favour women, while in another society it is the opposite.

Sometimes a man is angry that the law favours his wife and children, for example, in divorce arrangements. When this happens in our culture, the wife can be also be angry because, having gained custody of the children, she has to spend more time looking after them while her husband is free to make more money than her.

Without the knowledge of God, inequality causes anger and dissatisfaction. But the Word of God closes the gap. It removes impartiality and a sense of cheating. This is because we live and do all things in love.

Prayer

Spirit of fault-finding, I cast you out of my home and I send you to hell without returning, in Jesus' name.

Every evil memory operating through me or my partner against the purpose of God for my home, I use the blood of Jesus to cast you off, in Jesus' name.

Any record of evil stored in any place against my marriage, be destroyed by the fire of God, in Jesus' name.

Any power or spirit that steals liberty from my home, you shall fail in my life, in Jesus' name.

Every evil confession and imagination of either myself or my partner concerning our marriage, be nullified in Jesus' name.

Agent of perversion, fail in your mission against my home, in Jesus' name.

Every evil label in every area of my marriage be washed away by the blood of Jesus, in the name of Jesus.

Every anti-marriage yoke in operation in any area of my marriage be broken now by the anointing of the Holy Spirit, in Jesus' name.

I command any form of spiritual coldness in my marriage to receive the fire of the Holy Spirit, in Jesus' name.

Any evil eye monitoring the affairs of my home, I command you to go blind, in Jesus' name.

4

Pressure at Home

> "*For God hath not given us the spirit of fear; but of power, and of love, and of a sound mind.*"
> **2 Timothy 1:7**

God has given us a sound mind. A man of sound mind exercises self-control and discipline. He is able to think rightly and exhibit divine wisdom. If you are able to maintain a sound mind, you will be able to get many things right in your marriage.

Satan is constantly seeking an opportunity to attack your sound mind so that you will act irrationally in many situations.

Pressure is one of the major avenues Satan exploits to attack your sound mind. He builds pressure on you so that your mind will not function perfectly under many situations.

Today, homes are under continual attack because the couples have lost their mind due to unbearable pressure.

What is pressure?

It is a compelling or constraining influence such as a moral force on the mind (designed to make a person think or reason in a certain way) or will (designed to make a person conform or act in certain way).

Generally, pressure is an oppressive condition which could generate physical, mental, social or economic distress. When this pressure takes hold of us, it makes us act foolishly and do things that we would not have done naturally. This is because the sound mind has been lost or deactivated. Satan will always take advantage of any potential situation that could be used to generate pressure at home, so that the partners misbehave and possibly destroy their homes.

The sources of pressure on a home can be divided into two sections: internal and external.

A. Internal Source

This source produces pressure on you due to your personal moral weaknesses. It includes the following:

1. A MAN-PLEASING SPIRIT

This is a natural impulse in someone that makes him or her always says 'yes' to every demand from other people. When people discover that you don't know how to say no to them, they take advantage of you and keep coming to you with every demand – no matter how senseless it maybe.

Requests will keep on coming from relatives, friends, peers, etc. Your man-pleasing spirit makes you want to meet people's needs at the expense of your home. This spirit makes you deprive your own children and spouse in order to satisfy other people's needs. The end result of this action is pressure on every member of the home, including you. Satan will take advantage of your unrestricted, gullible kindness to cause trouble in your home, unless you start making your home your priority.

2. A MISPLACED PRIORITY

This is a weakness that makes you get your priorities wrong in your home. You will generate pressure on your marriage if you prioritise the little things that could be done later, and put off the big things that should be done first. Do not chase the minor at the expense of the major. Get your priorities right.

In Luke 10:38-42, Mary got her priorities right, while Martha got hers wrong. Martha then came under pressure. A misplaced priority can open the door to satanic invasion of your home. If you chase what you are not yet ready for, you will expose yourself and home to avoidable pressure.

3. Extravagance

This is a life of prodigality. It causes living beyond your means. The end result is financial mismanagement at home. Extravagance invites debts, if not dealt with urgently. The consequence of this is financial pressure due to huge debt or waste. Do not live beyond your means, otherwise you will drag your home into financial chaos and allow Satan to attack your marriage and family.

4. Unregulated Ambition

This weakness makes a man want to achieve big things within too short a period. The whole family will be dragged into the consequences of chasing unrealistic dreams and visions. The spouse that falls into this trap ignorantly pursues ambition he or she is not ready for. It is caused by impatience. Ambition that is not regulated by the Spirit of God will mess up the home and cause unreasonable pain. This opens a door to Satan to manipulate the agenda of your home. You must control your ambitions so that you will not drag your home into avoidable suffering.

5. Envy

This moral weakness generates unhealthy competition between people. It makes a man lose his originality in life. Such a person chases the dream of another home. He or she always wants his or her home to be like somebody else's home, even when there is no way that can be achieved.

If you always look towards another marriage to design yours, you will be running the race of another man. You will drag your home into a race it was not designed for and chase the plan of another marriage. The end result is pressure. This is because the situation in your home is not right for what you are chasing.

"For where envying and strife is, there is confusion and every evil work."

James 3:16

People under pressure are confused and disoriented. They have lost their sound minds.

6. INSENSITIVITY TO TIME CHANGE.

It is difficult to put new wine inside an old wine bottle. There will always be a need to adjust to changes. A home passes through different stages in life. There could be a time of lack or of abundance. There could be time of strength or of weakness. Your home must adjust to the situation of the new day.

For example, it will be difficult to maintain the same taste and lifestyle when there is a significant reduction in the finances of the home. When one of the spouses has lost a source of income the home must adjust to fit into the new day. Refusal to adjust will create pressure on every member of the home. Be sensitive to changes at home and make the necessary adjustment to avoid avoidable pressure. Otherwise, Satan will exploit the problem to create trouble in your relationship with your spouse.

B. External Source

This is the pressure that comes from external forces. These include:

1. Expectations

People around you have certain expectations from you. These people include parents, friends, peers, siblings, colleagues, etc. The expectation could be monetary or certain personal benefits. When they discover a delay in the realisation of their expectation, they may start building pressure on you. They may draw in more close associates of yours to join them in building pressure on you, so that you yield to their expectation.

Similarly, the society you belong to may have certain expectations of you. They may think that you are supposed to have gone far beyond the level of achievement that you have currently reached. They may start pressurising you to wake up and chase more goals in life. If you listen to their unwise criticism, you may be deceived into allowing their expectations to push you too hard or too fast in the journey of life, which will build up pressure on your home.

It is your responsibility to ensure that the interests of your home come first, and not the expectations of people. You must not yield or transfer this pressure to your marriage. If your marriage comes under attack due to the pressure you suffer, you will have foolishly dragged your home into danger.

2. The past

Your past mistakes can come back to haunt you and build pressure on you. For example, any undisclosed secret of your past before marriage can invite pressure on you, when you notice that the secret is about to come to the knowledge of your spouse.

In *Genesis 32:7-8*, Jacob came under pressure, including the whole family, because his past was returning to haunt him. In order to avoid your past putting pressure on you, disclose all your secrets to your spouse. Let him or her know everything about you. Otherwise, you will open a door to Satan to use your past to threaten your marriage.

3. Unfinished jobs

If you often abandon plans, fail to finish projects or give up on dreams, you may be creating future tensions in your home.

You may find yourself under pressure to complete a project you have abandoned in the past, and unfortunately you may no longer be in a good position to finish it. The situation in your home may not be able to accommodate such demands. This may build up pressure on you.

It is wise not to start what you can't complete, otherwise you may cause unwelcome distress in your marriage in the future. Don't delay till tomorrow what you can finish today, because you may not be in a suitable position to finish it when tomorrow comes.

4. Work

You need to have a good income, but work should not become a source of pressure on your marriage. You must regulate and control the demands of your work, otherwise it can generate unbearable pressure on your home. Work should not take up most of your time and energy; neither should it pull your marriage apart. Be wise.

Symptoms of pressure at home

The following are some signs that suggest that your home is under pressure:

1. Emotional imbalance

This generates irrational behaviour, either through yourself or your spouse. Pressure causes people to behave unreasonably.

This is because they have lost the soundness of their mind. Such people get angry quickly and become easily irritated, especially when someone opposes their views or expresses a criticism. They become unfriendly. Worry, anger and anxiety creep into their mind. If the situation is not quickly dealt with, the person may fall into depression.

2. Lawlessness

A home under pressure becomes disordered and lawless. Individual members of the home will lose their moral shape, and treat each other without respect. Family law is violated and there is no clear mutual direction in the family members' lives. They are dragged into sinful practices. They disobey God and break family agreements.

3. Tension

People under pressure live under tension. The atmosphere at home is tense and there is no peaceful co-existence.

4. High-handedness

Homes under pressure live under oppression. People behave unfairly towards each other. The strongest person in the home dominates the other members and forces them to do what he/she wants.

5. Double personalities

People under pressure begin to live in two worlds. They stop being real. Individuals display different personalities to different people, as they are trying to please certain people due to the pressure they put on them. For example, a woman under pressure to please her mother at the expense of her marriage will show one personality before her mother, and another one before her husband. Lying and deception become common practice.

6. INDIVIDUALISM

In a home under pressure, individual members will be struggling to find their feet in order to forge ahead. Pressure disunites a home. Individuals begin to think of themselves rather than others, due to insecurity and fear. People become self-seeking and individualistic, both in thinking and action.

Prolonged pressure

If the situation at home is not quickly normalised and pressure removed, the following become inevitable:

1. PERMANENT CHARACTER DEFORMATION

Members of the family get used to bad habits. As long as the pressure remains, people can never escape its effects. Wrong behaviour becomes a lifestyle.

2. SPIRITUAL RETARDATION

Homes under continual pressure will suffer spiritually. Members may stop praying together due to incessant character deformation. This may bring an end to the family altar. Their spiritual life may come under demonic attack.

3. DEMONIC STRONGHOLD

Continual error will receive demonic attention that becomes a stronghold in the family. Whenever a wrong situation is allowed to persist, demons will highjack it and turn it into a stronghold. When this happens, strife and an unhealthy atmosphere become the order of the day at home. The end result is an invitation to affliction. Such a home may start experiencing a strange sickness, or unusual kinds of hardship and abnormality.

Dealing with pressure at home

It is better to avoid pressure at home, but if it happens, here's what you should do:

1. IDENTIFY THE SOURCE OF THE PRESSURE

Prayerfully identify where the pressure is coming from and deal with it wisely. If it is your job, address the matter without delay. If it is your parents, handle it with caution. If it is your spouse, deal with it patiently.

2. COMMUNICATE

The two partners should jointly address the matter. They should come together and talk about the pressure in their home. They should face the situation in a united way. There should be no pointing of fingers. Communication should be based on the Bible – the infallible Word of God. The Holy Spirit should be allowed to bring conviction of the mind to each of the spouses.

3. PRAY

The couple should pray for peace, understanding and the conviction of the Holy Spirit, so that the spouse responsible for the pressure at home can be convinced. Prayer should also be made for discretion and the ability to judge the situation rightly. Pray that all external influences damaging the relationship between you and your spouse will be terminated by God. Return to the family altar.

Any source generating evil pressure on my home, I command you to dry up now, in Jesus' name.

I decree that the power and spirit of error shall fail in my home, in Jesus' name.

Father, remove any evil anointing that promotes wastefulness from my life and that of my spouse, in Jesus' name.

Father, deliver me from every moral weakness in my life that would frustrate my marriage today, in Jesus' name.

I reject every false vision, dream and pursuit for my marriage, in the name of Jesus.

If there is a river of bitterness flowing in my heart towards my spouse or flowing in my spouse's heart towards me, Father, let it dry up today, in Jesus' name.

Father, any tree in my marriage that you have not planted, root it out today, in Jesus' name.

Whatever may be sponsoring separation in my marriage, may it fall and die now, in Jesus' name.

Father, dispel every kind of tension in my marriage, in Jesus' name.

I decree that my home shall not get its priorities wrong, in Jesus' name.

5

The Spirit of Individualism

This is a spirit from hell that attacks the unity of a home. It causes partners to live the life of individuals, even though they are married. This spirit advocates self-reliance and personal independence. This spirit makes the husband and wife live as separate entities under the same roof.

"And they twain shall be one flesh: so then they are no more twain, but one flesh. What therefore God hath joined together, let not man put asunder."

Mark 10:8-9

Husbands and wives are supposed to be one in all things. This is the only thing that guarantees the future of their union. Jesus warns that no one should separate what God has joined together. This implies that there is a possibility of a husband and wife splitting up. And a couple can be separated while still living together, when individualism creeps into their relationship.

Symptoms of individualism at home include the following:

1. LACK OF MUTUAL SUBMISSION

Ephesians 5:21 advocates mutual submission in marriage. When a couple becomes individualistic, the partners don't submit to each other. Two governments will be formed at home: one headed by each spouse. The individuals pursue their own dreams and live for themselves rather than thinking of their partner.

2. Pursuit of different purposes in life

The husband and wife will pursue different agendas and plans. They will have no common purpose.

3. Marital competition

The husband and wife will engage in competition between themselves. They turn their home into a race track where they compete against each other.

4. Contentious relationship

The couple will always live in disagreement. The husband and wife argue over almost everything. This is because they operate with conflicting vision and purpose. If you notice that you and your spouse are always in disagreement over every issue, it maybe that you are practising individualism.

5. Loss of sympathy

When the individual is the focus, you don't even see the misery of your partner. Individualism erodes sympathy.

6. Selfishnes

The individual spouse thinks only of him or herself. Each seeks only his or her own good.

The open doors

"Neither give place to the devil."

Ephesians 4:27

You give place to the devil in your marriage when you drift into carnality in handling the affairs of your home. When personal weaknesses take control of you, the devil will gain access to manipulate your situation.

The open doors to the spirit of individualism are:

1. DISCONTENTMENT

When a partner is not satisfied with the situation in the marriage, the person may fall into deception – thinking that individualism will make life better.

"Let your conversation be without covetousness; and be content with such things as ye have: for he hath said, I will never leave thee, nor forsake thee."

Hebrews 13:5

2. SELF-CENTREDNESS

A dissatisfied partner makes him or herself the focus. The person considers only his or her own needs and ignores those of their partner. Selfishness opens the door to the spirit of individualism.

3. SELF-CONFIDENCE

This creeps in when a partner starts believing in himself or herself instead of the combined effort of the two of them. Such a person starts seeing the partner as the one dragging back and slowing him or her down in the journey of life. The self-confident person then chooses to do it alone.

"He that trusteth in his own heart is a fool: but whoso walketh wisely, he shall be delivered."

Proverbs 28:26

4. LACK OF ADJUSTMENT

Marriage requires adjustments. When a married person still wants to live as a single person, the person will fall into individualism, planning and doing his or her own things alone without involving the other partner. Marriage requires a life lived jointly and shared together. You can't do things alone when you're married.

Consequences

When partners allow individualism in their relationship, the Holy Spirit withdraws the blessings of unity in the home.

"Behold, how good and how pleasant it is for brethren to dwell together in unity! It is like the precious ointment upon the head, that ran down upon the beard, even Aaron's beard: that went down to the skirts of his garments; as the dew of Hermon, and as the dew that descended upon the mountains of Zion: for there the LORD commanded the blessing, even life for evermore."

Psalm 133:1-3

This psalm indicates that when the children of God dwell together in unity, the Lord causes certain blessings to flow into their midst.

In such a home, there will be harmony, strength and prosperity. But if there is no unity, the opposite of blessings is imminent. God never dwells in a disordered place, neither will He bless disorder. Similarly, the blessing of unity could manifest in terms of empowerment. Grace is released to empower an individual or the couple to reach certain heights that would have been impossible with only their natural ability. Unfortunately, if there is no unity, the grace is withdrawn and the ability to rise to greater heights is hindered.

Furthermore, disunity will rob partners of the blessing of living together as a couple, as the writer of Ecclesiastes said:

"Two are better than one; because they have a good reward for their labour. For if they fall, the one will lift up his fellow: but woe to him that is alone

when he falleth; for he hath not another to help him up. Again, if two lie together, then they have heat: but how can one be warm alone? And if one prevail against him, two shall withstand him; and a threefold cord is not quickly broken."

Ecclesiastes 4:9-12

These verses show the benefits of unity that a disunited couple will lose:

1. BETTER HARVEST

The labour of two people will yield a better result where there is unity. When two people come together to build for a common purpose, they will do better than doing it individually. But disunity will cause a poor harvest. The effort of one person will yield little.

2. RESTORATION

If one falls, the other can help to restore him or her back to their former position. When one falls, the one standing will stretch out their hands to lift the other up. But where there is no unity, the partner that falls may not be able to get up again.

3. BETTER FELLOWSHIP

They warm each other. They pray, study the Bible together and worship God together. Where two or three gather in God's name, the Lord is in their midst. You can't fellowship alone.

4. BETTER RESISTANCE

They have more strength together. Two people can resist the devil better than one. They can fight the enemy better. Individualism will make you face the battle of life alone. Due to your little strength, you will be vulnerable if you fight the enemy alone.

Coming out of individualism

1. Take Responsibility for Your Actions

Do not justify your negative behaviour by blaming it on your spouse. Accept that you are wrong to promote disunity in your marriage, irrespective of what might have been the causes.

2. Communicate with Your Spouse

Avoid accusations and finger-pointing. Choose the position of peace-maker in your home. Be the first to raise the difficulty in your marriage with your spouse. Talk through the situation. Seek out a Spirit-filled counsellor for better clarification.

3. Prayerfully Examine Yourself

Let the Holy Spirit illuminate your mind to see your faults.

4. Jointly Address All the Actions of Individualism in Your Relationship

Write down all your problems together. Develop an action plan to tackle them.

5. Jointly Create a Plan for How to Avoid the Recurrence of Disunity in Your Marriage

Whenever things go wrong in a relationship, both individuals involved have contributed directly or indirectly. Therefore, the issue is not going to be who is right or wrong, or who is to blame or not. Both people have their own share of the wrongs. There is no need to apportion the blame, but each person must allow the Holy Spirit to illuminate his or her mind to see their personal weaknesses. To come out of a wrong situation, there will always be a need for a change of attitude.

I pray that every secret of the devil in your marriage shall be exposed and defeated, in Jesus' name.

I command any power hardening the heart of my partner or myself to die, in the name of Jesus.

Every hindrance to restoration in my home, disappear now in Jesus' name.

May the fire of God consume any weed hindering the harvest of joy in my home right now, in Jesus' name.

Every wall of separation erected between me and my spouse, collapse now, in Jesus' name.

Father, let your Spirit breathe abundant life upon my home, in Jesus' name.

Attacker of my marital success, I command you to fall and die now, in Jesus' name.

I reject and disgrace any satanic report and judgement concerning my marriage, in Jesus' name.

Every wile and device of the devil against my marriage shall not prosper, in Jesus' name.

In the name of Jesus, I command to enter into captivity, any power or spirit assigned from hell to kill potentials and virtues God has deposited in my marriage.

Every manifestation of the spirit of selfishness in my marriage, be cancelled now by the blood of Jesus.

5

Attack on Communication

Communication is the process of transferring a message between a sender and a receiver. The message could be a piece of information, a feeling or an idea. It is impossible for a marriage to succeed without effective communication.

When people involved in a relationship stop communicating, their relationship starts to die. When a couple experience prolonged communication problems, it will not be long before they separate.

The devil will always attempt to create a communication barrier or breakdown in a marriage, because he knows that when communication suffers in any relationship, such a relationship will soon die.

The devil will attack the communication in a marriage usually by exploiting certain weaknesses in the lives of the partners to cause friction. Their bad attitudes become an open door to communication problems.

Examples of such bad attitudes that can serve as an open door to communication deterioration include the following:

1. ASSERTIVENESS

This manifests in the form of aggression and insistence. A partner suffering from this attitude will always insist that his or her opinion should be respected above the other partner. Aggression will be shown that will frighten the other partner to make him or her to submit to the view being promoted. If this attitude continues in communication, the devil may influence the spouse on the receiving end to avoid communication, preferring to be silent rather than discuss issues. If you notice this in your spouse, you may need to check your manner of talking.

1 Corinthians 9:25 says: *"And every man that striveth for the mastery is temperate in all things."* Learn how to be temperate in your communication.

Avoid being aggressive and assertive. Respect the opinion of your spouse.

2. ARGUMENTATIVE

This attitude sponsors contentious, combative and belligerent behaviour during communication. The person suffering from this spirit always sees things from a different angle and is fond of turning discussions into arguments. He or she rarely accepts opposing ideas freely. Every opinion from their partner is criticised without close examination. An argumentative person refuses to accept the rational conclusion that results from a discussion.

If you have this attitude, it may open a door to the devil to manipulate your partner to avoid engaging you in any matter that needs deliberation. Your spouse will start operating alone as a way of maintaining peace. When you notice this in your spouse, you will need to talk it over and explore why you always show such a bad attitude. If your spouse is the argumentative one, make it known to your spouse that this is a bad attitude that inhibits your communication.

Proverbs 21:19 says: *"It is better to dwell in the wilderness, than with a contentious and an angry woman"!* The same applies with contentious men. Unreasonable arguing is a reflection of dislike towards what somebody has said. Avoid it. It is dangerous.

3. Domineering

This spirit produces imbalance during communication because only one party will do most of the talking. The other person will be a mere observer while the domineering person is busy talking. This spirit operates through the person who considers himself or herself as having better ideas. Such a person does most of the talking in order to promote those ideas.

If this attitude is a continual characteristic of communication, the home will be ruled by the opinions of only one person in the marriage. The interests of the other person will be marginalised, since his or her views are not given any positive consideration. It is only a matter of time before the spouse of the domineering person will lose motivation in discussions, especially in conversations where certain decisions need to be taken. At this point, the devil may exploit the situation to promote communication breakdown.

4. Repetition

This spirit manifests through repetition of statements or words. The person suffering from this spirit will keep on saying the same thing over and over again during communication. Some people use it to convey the seriousness of their message, while some use it to hint that they are not prepared to negotiate or compromise on the matter under discussion. Repetition makes communication boring and monotonous. It may open a door to the devil making your spouse appear uninterested and slow to respond during communication.

5. Exaggeration

This operates to mislead the listener in some way, or to draw sympathy. Exaggeration is just a subtle word for lying.

THE ENEMY OF *Marriage*

Proverbs 17:4 says: *"A wicked doer giveth heed to false lips; and a liar giveth ear to a naughty tongue."* Exaggeration is a lie and it is of the devil. You should stop it in your communication. The more you exaggerate, the more you lie and the more you give the devil a chance to intervene in your marriage matters, because the devil delights in deception.

6. LYING SPIRIT

This spirit helps people cover up the truth. Due to the fear of being rebuked or humiliated, a spouse may lie during communication in order to conceal the truth.

You lie to your spouse because you don't want the truth to be known. Sometimes your spouse will act ignorantly based on the lie you have told, and this will later result in disaster. When your spouse discovers that he or she has acted under deceptive words from you, your word will no longer be respected in the family. The devil may then manipulate his or her mind never to trust your word again. This may be the beginning of continual communication problems.

7. CRITICISM

This act encourages judgement and accusation during communication. A spouse suffering from the critical spirit will fault every word spoken by his or her partner. Your conversation will be laced with criticism. Soon your partner will start feeling uncomfortable and unfairly judged, and will become antagonistic in return. If the situation persists, there will be a communication breakdown at home. The devil then exploits the situation to cause more serious problems in the relationship.

8. UNYIELDING

This attitude makes a person unwilling to change their position on an issue, even when it is clear that the opinion of the other person is better than his or her own. The person blindly holds onto his or her own opinions, irrespective of the fact that they are unpopular or plainly wrong.

If you always insist that your opinion is right, and you are not prepared to shift your ground, your spouse may resort to individualism. This means that he or she does things in his or her own way, without consulting you. At this stage, the devil may hijack the situation to create more obstacles in the marriage. It is important to stop being stupidly rigid.

9. WORD-TWISTING

This is an attitude that causes wrong interpretations of what is being said. A person that suffers from it will often give the wrong meaning to the word spoken by his or her partner. People like this are easily offended, because they interpret the words of their partner as insulting or critical, when in fact their partner has no such intention.

Psalm 56:5 says: *"Every day they wrest my words: all their thoughts are against me for evil."* In this verse, 'wrest' means twist, like a wrestler tries to twist his opponent onto the floor. Spoken words are given a different meaning by the hearer. This can either be a very subtle difference or a completely opposite meaning. Either way it can be harmful. The devil may exploit the situation to make the other partner avoid any depth of conversation due to the fear of being misinterpreted or misquoted.

10. DISTRACTION

This spirit sponsors the manifestation of past hurts into the present discussion. Bitter words spoken in the past are brought into the present communication. Your partner reminds you of offences or negative comments you have made in the past, in order to undermine whatever point you are making. This complicates what is being discussed in the present and opens a door to the devil to cause a breakdown in communication.

11. Arrogance

This habit provokes disrespectful words during communication. Communication with an arrogant person will be filled with insults and intimidation. An arrogant spouse ridicules the opinion of their partner and exalts his or her own opinion. Soon, the devil exploits the situation to sponsor anger and irritation, which leads to communication problems.

12. Impatience

This weakness makes the speaker demand an immediate answer in a matter that actually needs a longer period of critical thinking.

The person pressurises his or her spouse into giving instant opinions and answers on very serious or complex matters. If the partner of an impatient person yields to the pressure and gives a response when ideas have not been well thought through, the home will be heading for disaster due to a wrong decision. If the partner of a person with a weakness for impatience refuses to yield to the pressure to give an urgent answer, their action will be wrongly interpreted by the impatient person. This opens a door to the devil to cause friction in the relationship, which may well hinder communication.

To overcome or prevent communication problems, apply the following biblical guidance:

1. The Tongue of the Learned

"The Lord GOD hath given me the tongue of the learned, that I should know how to speak a word in season to him that is weary: he wakeneth morning by morning, he wakeneth mine ear to hear as the learned."

Isaiah 50:4

The tongue of the learned is the wisdom of knowing what to say, which comes from studying God's Word. It will help you know how to talk and reply to every comment you receive from your spouse, to bring encouragement, comfort, peace and all good things. With this tongue, your word will always be approved by God.

Prayer point: Father, please give me the tongue of the learned. Help me to know how to talk in every situation, in Jesus' name.

2. RESTRAINED LIPS

"In the multitude of words there wanteth not sin: but he that refraineth his lips is wise."

Proverbs 10:19

Restrained lips are those that control what is said. Someone who is in control of their tongue is always brief in their words. Don't open your mouth without thinking about what you are saying first. Many arguments has been caused by hasty words.

If you talk too much, you can become irritating to your spouse. And the more you say, the greater the risk of being misinterpreted by your spouse. So choose your words carefully, and don't wear your partner out by 'talking them to death'! There are also times when you should keep your mouth shut. Some words are not for sharing, as they may do more harm than good.

Prayer point: Father, please give me the grace to control my lips. Perfect my speech in all situations, in Jesus' name.

3. EVIL WORDS

"Let all bitterness, and wrath, and anger, and clamour, and evil speaking, be put away from you, with all malice…"

Ephesians 4:31

A man with an evil heart has an evil tongue. His words betray his character. So the first task is to grow our relationship with God, so that there will be no evil in our hearts to overflow out of our mouths. But even the holiest of people are tempted to say bad things, so we must keep a tight rein on our lips.

If you can stop yourself from speaking evil words, you will avoid hurting your spouse and prevent arguments with him or her.

Prayer point: Father, please fill my mouth with good words, in Jesus' name. Make me a man/woman of clean lips.

4. OFFENSIVE WORDS

"For in many things we offend all. If any man offend not in word, the same is a perfect man, and able also to bridle the whole body."

James 3:2

Offensive words create fights at home because they annoy and antagonise your spouse. If your words make your spouse angry, you need to change.

Prayer point: Father, please remove offensive words from my mouth and help me to always be pleasant in conversation.

5. GUILELESS WORDS

"For he that will love life, and see good days, let him refrain his tongue from evil, and his lips that they speak no guile: Let him eschew evil, and do good; let him seek peace, and ensue it."

1 Peter 3:10-11

A guileless word is a sincere word that has no deception. Avoid speaking a deceptive word to your spouse because you can *"be sure your sin will find you out" (Numbers 32:23.)*, and one day that word will be exposed. The result will be that you will lose respect and integrity in your spouse's eyes. Your spouse will develop a negative attitude towards you in communication.

Prayer point: Father, please make me a lover of peace and fill my mouth with words that promote life.

6. WISE WORDS

"The mouth of the righteous speaketh wisdom, and his tongue talketh of judgment."

Psalm 37:30

A wise man speaks wisely and his words give direction. In this verse, the tongue that talks of "judgement" does not mean criticising others, it means that a wise person says what is just or correct. Your word is supposed to bring solutions to a problem, not make the matter worse.

Prayer point: Father, please make me a speaker of wise words and let my tongue bring solutions in all situations.

7. PROMOTER OF JUSTICE

"The law of truth was in his mouth, and iniquity was not found in his lips: he walked with me in peace and equity, and did turn many away from iniquity."

Malachi 2:6

A promoter of justice is the person who is impartial in conversation, and always speaks what is true. His word also promotes repentance, because when he speaks, the receiver sees what is wrong in his own life. Veils are removed through his word. We turn people away from "iniquity" not by condemnation but by *"speaking the truth in love" (Ephesians 4:15)*.

Prayer point: Father, please make me an agent of justice and put words in my mouth that give understanding.

THE ENEMY OF Marriage

8. Heart of Understanding

"Understanding is a wellspring of life unto him that hath it: but the instruction of fools is folly."

Proverbs 16:22

A heart of understanding will help you to foresee the reaction of your spouse to your style of communication. You will know what to say and what not to say in order to avoid communication breakdown. Your word will not cause emotional disturbance because you avoid certain attitudes during communication. You will know how to talk when your spouse is not in a good mood and what to say when he or she is in high spirits.

Prayer point: Father, please give me a heart of understanding so that I can live peaceably with my spouse.

9. Think before you talk

"The heart of the wise teacheth his mouth, and addeth learning to his lips."

Proverbs 16:23

Your heart can only teach your mouth how to speak if you think before you speak. Thinking before speaking will enable you to speak from a heart of love and not from negative emotions like anger, jealousy or selfishness. The Holy Spirit whispers the correct, gentle words in our hearts, but if we let our emotions rule our lips, we will speak before we have listened to the Spirit. If you can be patient and slow to speak, you will take control of your words. Avoid speaking hastily because your mouth will be fed by the emotions of your human soul, not your spiritual heart.

Prayer point: Father, please give me a gentle spirit in communication.

10. Pleasant words

"Pleasant words are as an honeycomb, sweet to the soul, and health to the bones."

Proverbs 16:24

A speaker of pleasant words is an encourager. His word gives strength to the weak. When such a person speaks to a broken heart, the heart is mended. When your spouse is discouraged and afraid, he or she needs words that give hope and increase faith. Be sensitive to your spouse's situation and let your words meet their immediate needs.

Prayer point: Father, please make me a speaker of words that give life and promote faith, in Jesus' name.

11. United home

"That ye may with one mind and one mouth glorify God, even the Father of our Lord Jesus Christ."

Romans 15:6

A home that is united is one where couples reason and think alike. And if they differ on a subject, it is one where they defer to each other and put their partner's feelings first. But where faith is concerned, they have similar opinions concerning all situations, because they are one with each other and Christ Jesus. The more they become like Him, the more they will be like each other, because they are both learning to imitate Him.

Unity promotes effective communication in marriage. United minds understand each other easily. They speak as one in all important situations. Couples who have been happily married for many years often know what the other one is thinking before they open their mouths, and can finish their spouse's sentence for them (though, doing that too often can be irritating!).

Communication breakdown results from a diversity of opinions, with an individual rigidly attached to his or her own opinions, unwilling to shift ground.

Prayer point: Father, please unite me and my spouse in both thought and action. Make us one indeed.

12. Seasoned speech

"Let your speech be always with grace, seasoned with salt, that ye may know how ye ought to answer every man."

Colossians 4:6

Seasoned words edify the hearer. They are attractive. Let your speech be fit for the occasion. Speak words that give direction, not confusion. You will be able to speak with grace if you always consider the other person's feelings before opening your mouth. Then your answer will be right for the other person, 'leaving a good taste in their mouth' rather than a trail of bitterness or resentment.

Prayer point: Father, please teach me how to use my tongue properly. Make me a speaker of words that build people up rather than tearing them down.

13. Simple declaration

"But let your communication be, Yea, yea; Nay, nay: for whatsoever is more than these cometh of evil."

Matthew 5:37

Let your conversation be simple. Make speech that is easy to understand. Use words that your spouse will quickly comprehend. Also, be a person of integrity in communication so that your spouse trusts your word all the time, which will mean you won't have to swear an oath to establish the truth of a particular statement to your spouse.

Prayer point: Lord, please help me to speak plainly so that there will be no confusion in communication with my marriage partner.

14. WAR OF WORDS

"The mouth of a righteous man is a well of life: but violence covereth the mouth of the wicked."

Proverbs 10:11

The word of threat and fear breeds strife. It leads to violence at home. Avoid threatening your spouse during communication. A home where the couple engage in a war of words will not have peace. There will always be uncertainty and heartache.

Prayer point: Dear Father, may I never threaten my partner nor make him/her feel afraid of me, in Jesus' name.

15. SOUND SPEECH

"Sound speech that cannot be condemned; that he that is of the contrary part may be ashamed, having no evil thing to say of you."

Titus 2:8

Soundness of speech means honesty and telling the truth, and words that are hard to fault. Avoid giving an untruthful reply in response to harsh words from your spouse. If your spouse speaks nastily to you, avoid replying in the same style. Don't repay evil for evil (Romans 12:17). Maintain the soundness of your speech in all situations. Soon, you will win your spouse over. Two wrongs can never make a right.

Prayer point: Lord God, may my speech always be sound, so that it may never be the cause of strife.

16. STAY WITH THE TRUTH

"Hold fast the form of sound words, which thou hast heard of me, in faith and love which is in Christ Jesus."

2 Timothy 1:13

In all your conversations with your spouse, maintain speaking the right word and don't drift into the bad language of the world. You must avoid words that conflict with the gospel. Hold fast to the right word, irrespective of what your spouse is saying to you. By doing so, you will create room for the Holy Spirit to convict your spouse and change his or her behaviour.

Prayer point: Keep my lips in line with your Word, dear Lord.

Communication redundancy be terminated in my home, in Jesus' name.

Father, please bring divine correction to every evil advice that myself or my spouse have ever received that has brought trouble into our home.

Seed of pride and arrogance, die and leave me now, in Jesus' name.

Father, whatever in me or my spouse that may make my marriage a failure, remove it today, in Jesus' name.

I decree that the spirit that twists words shall not prosper in my home, in Jesus' name.

Argumentative spirit, you shall not reign in my marriage, in Jesus' name.

Father, I surrender my tongue to you, circumcise it, in Jesus' name.

Every evil prophecy spoken by any tongue into my marriage shall not stand, in Jesus' name.

Father, please unite me and my spouse in thought and action, in Jesus' name.

I disconnect my home from any form of evil connection, in Jesus' name.

7

Strife

Strife is an attack on the peaceful coexistence in marriage. When couples engage in strife, Satan can take advantage of the situation to cause separation or divorce. If a couple can prevent strife in their relationship, they will enjoy the free flow of God's blessings.

I'm devoting a significant amount of space to this topic to give couples a detailed understanding of the impact of strife on their common destiny.

Symptoms of strife in a home

1. FIGHTS

These could be physical, such as hitting each other. They could also be emotional, such as torturing each other by denial of sex and other basic emotional needs. Conflict could also be verbal, using vindictive or threatening words. Or a fight could be psychological, for example, the silent use of aggressive or offensive body language, like the flashing of malicious facial expressions to irritate each other.

2. Individualism

This is a situation whereby each partner does his or her own things. There is no common purpose and no sharing of lives. Each individual pursues his or her own destiny separately.

3. Rivalry

This manifests as competition. Whatever one spouse does, the other spouse will also do it, and attempt to do it better. The two partners compete for glory in their relationship, probably to prove a point to each other. This is strife.

4. Heated Argument

This is a lack of agreement and unity in marriage. The couple always act and reason in opposition. They argue over all things, never uniting over anything. Their incessant argument will result in communication breakdown. This is a symptom of strife.

5. Dishonour

Couples engulfed in strife lack mutual respect in their relationship. Negative treatment and physical or verbal abuse is a common occurrence in such a home. There is contempt and disparagement.

Major causes of strife

A couple are drifting into strife when the devil exploits their personal weaknesses and uses those to lure them into friction. Examples of such weaknesses include:

1. Character defects

Personal weaknesses are the major reason why couples end up in strife. These include:

a. Hatred

Proverbs 10:12 says that *"hatred stirreth up strifes: but love covereth all sins."*

If you get easily irritated by your spouse's error, or something you hate about them, strife is almost certain to follow. The root of hatred could be lack of acceptability. If there is a something your spouse just can't accept about you, there will always be conflict.

b. Contentiousness

Proverbs 26:21 says that just *"as coals are to burning coals, and wood to fire; so is a contentious man to kindle strife."*

A contentious man is someone who argues over everything; he has an argumentative spirit. Such a person always starts a conversation by opposing what has just been said. Such people are unwilling to accept the views of others, no matter how reasonable they seem. This may make the contentious person's partner angry, and if that is not properly managed, it may well result in strife.

c. Wrath

Proverbs 15:18 says that *"a wrathful man stirreth up strife: but he that is slow to anger appeaseth strife."*

A wrathful man is a man full of anger. Such people easily lose their temper; any little disagreement turns into a heated argument. Anger is infectious. An angry spouse will soon produce an angry partner. The home will be ruled by rage. The spirit of strife then invades the marriage.

d. Perverseness

Proverbs 16:28 says that *"a froward man soweth strife: and a whisperer separateth chief friends."*

THE ENEMY OF Marriage

A froward man is one who acts perversely. Such a person deliberately acts contrary to what is agreed or considered normal. He or she is always bending the rules, and will agree on something with the spouse and then change the plan without telling the spouse. This makes the other person feel like a fool. Soon, there will be quarrels, arguments and strife.

e. Sin

Proverbs 17:19 says, "He loveth transgression that loveth strife: and he that exalteth his gate seeketh destruction."

Sin is lawlessness and it breeds strife. Wherever there is a sin, the devil has the legal right to be present, because he is the author of sin. A home where sin reigns can never be at peace. Sin opens the door to demonic invasion into the home.

f. Scorn

Proverbs 22:10 says, "Cast out the scorner, and contention shall go out; yea, strife and reproach shall cease."

A scorner is a mocker. Mockery will make your spouse feel stupid and will cause strife. Jokes and humour can be a good thing, but avoid sarcastic words. Avoid words that ridicule and make your partner feel worthless, otherwise, there will always be strife.

g. Pride

Proverbs 28:25 says, "He that is of a proud heart stirreth up strife: but he that putteth his trust in the lord shall be made fat."

A proud man behaves very selfishly because he cares only for himself. Such a person never says sorry when wrong, because he or she never accepts being wrong. In contrast, a proud person always demands an apology and respect from others. Soon, the spouse will rebel. Strife is imminent.

2. CARNALITY

Carnality (the passions and appetites of the sinful nature) breeds works of the flesh. For example, unbelief is a work of the flesh.

In *Genesis 16:1-6*, after God has promised Abraham and Sarah a son they decide to help that promise come true themselves. Through pressure from Sarah, Abraham succumbs to the dictates of the flesh. They have a child, but the child becomes a source of strife in their relationship.

It is a general consequence that whenever a couple agree to help themselves outside God's will for them, it is only a matter of time before there will be strife.

Flesh is of the devil and wherever the product of the devil is, he has the right to visit the place. The acts of the flesh will always cause strife because they give the devil the right to enter the relationship.

Romans 8:6 says, *"For to be carnally minded is death; but to be spiritually minded is life and peace."*

3. BLESSINGS

The more God blesses you, the more you should pray for wisdom to manage it as a married person. If not properly managed, ironically blessings can create tension and strife in the relationship.

In *Genesis 13:4-7*, due to the blessings of God in the lives of Lot and Abraham, the land could no longer accommodate them so competition came in – and there was strife. The more you are blessed, the more you want blessings.

As God begins to bless a couple, their tastes imperceptibly begin to change, ambitions change, plans change, lifestyles change and interests change.

The couple may also begin to have different views about themselves and each other in terms of personal identity. This causes a change in their expectations of each other, usually in terms of treatment and respect. If not properly managed, there could be conflicts of interest. Sometimes agreement can become difficult and, unknowingly to them, they enter into argument and strife sets in.

For example, the spouse that brings more money home may be tempted to start demanding a bigger share of the family's money, and consider himself or herself to have more rights over the family purse. The partner may even expect more respect from the other partner because more blessings come through him or her into the family. In some situations, the partner that brings in less money or material blessing into the home may start feeling intimidated, and this may invite dissatisfaction and strife.

It should be noted that whatever blessing any of the spouses bring into the home is from God and it is for the common purpose of the whole family.

4. Generational problems

A spirit of strife could be inherited from the bloodline.

Some homes are engulfed in strife not because the husband or wife is bad, but because one of them has an inheritance of strife from their bloodline – their parental lineage.

For example, in *Genesis 34:25*, Simeon and Levi took revenge because their sister, Dinah, was raped by some villagers. They killed all the men in the place.

From that time onwards there was a manifestation of the spirit of strife in their bloodline. In *Exodus 2:1-2*, we read that Moses was born from the bloodline of Levi, almost 500years later. In *Exodus 2:11-12*, Moses killed an Egyptian through strife and anger.

Similarly, in *Exodus 32:27-28*, the sons of Levi went into the camp to kill people with the sword (though, they did it to claim that they were on the God's side). In *Genesis 49:5-7*, strife robbed Simeon and Levi of their father's blessings because *"instruments of cruelty are in their habitations"* (verse 5) and *"in their anger they slew a man"* (verse 6).

There are some families or tribes or communities that are known for strife. Such people cannot control their anger or resist taking offence. Any disagreement or confrontation irritates them. It takes very little provocation for strife to start. Such people always have a reason to be vengeful and to separate from others. Until this evil inherited seed is removed from their life, it will be difficult to maintain a peaceful home.

If you notice that you find it difficult to manage emotions resulting from some offensive remark, and that you always think you have a good reason to engage in strife, you will need to take it to God for deliverance.

The impact of strife on marriage

Understanding the danger of strife will help you to avoid it in your marriage.

Whenever you notice strife in your relationship, remind yourself of the consequences it will have...

1. IT HINDERS THE WORK OF THE HOLY SPIRIT

"For the kingdom of God is not meat and drink; but righteousness, and peace, and joy in the Holy Ghost."

Romans 14:17

THE ENEMY OF *Marriage*

Strife will inhibit the ministry of the Holy Spirit in your home.

The Holy Spirit works in an atmosphere of peace, where people dwell together in the fear of God. The Holy Spirit works to fulfil the plans of God for your marriage. These plans include spiritual, physical and material blessings. But strife will hinder this possibility.

When you notice that your marriage is in hardship for too long, you may need to check whether your home is in strife. You will be delaying the plan of God for your home if you allow strife to dominate your marriage.

I pray that every seed of strife in your home shall die today, in Jesus' name.

2. IT CREATES DISORDER

"But if ye have bitter envying and strife in your hearts, glory not, and lie not against the truth. This wisdom descendeth not from above, but is earthly, sensual, devilish. For where envying and strife is, there is confusion and every evil work."

James 3:14-16

A home filled with strife will be brought into disorder.

Strife breeds disorder. Disorder breeds malfunctioning. That is, neither partner will be able to function well in their divine destiny. The situation at home will not be conducive for the divine supernatural to operate. Where there is disorder, darkness rules. People live under ignorance and are unable to see far in the journey of life. The ability to make right decisions is hindered. The couple mess up their common destiny.

I pray that the power that twists destiny shall fail in your home, in Jesus' name.

3. MUTUAL DESTRUCTION.

"But if ye bite and devour one another, take heed that ye be not consumed one of another."

Galatians 5:15

Where there is strife, people end up in mutual destruction of each other. That is, the devil hires them against each other.

During strife, people inflict pain and stress on each other. They may even attack each other, and the weakest among them maybe the first to feel the full impact of the blow. During strife, people speak evil words into each other's destiny. All these activities bring destruction into the lives of the partners, both as individuals and as a couple.

I pray that every assignment against your spouse that the devil has planned to give you shall fail, in Jesus' name.

How to avoid and escape strife.

To avoid or come out of strife will require both individual and joint decisions of the couple.

A. JOINT DECISIONS TO MAKE:

The couple should jointly decide to set rules such as these;

1. We shall never insult each other in this home.
2. We shall never raise our hands against each other in this home.
3. We shall never engage each other in a heated argument. When an argument is getting hot, somebody must be the first to stop.

4. We shall never sleep without settling an argument. That is, we shall never go to bed at night without settling an issue or controversy of the day. We shall never carry an offence into the second day.

5. We shall never refer again to an issue that was settled in the past. That is, we shall always treat the past as past.

6. We shall give praise for every apology. When there is an issue, the first to apologise will be praised in this home. We will always be quick to forgive each other.

7. We shall be each other's confidant. My spouse will be my best friend. That is, we shall never tell outsiders bad information about our partner or our marriage.

8. If there is a need for counselling, we shall ask only our pastor or a Spirit-filled person with proven integrity. We shall never report on each other to friends or in-laws or parents, because they will be sentimental and are unlikely to be impartial, and so add fuel to the fire.

9. We shall create an atmosphere of laughter in this home. We will laugh over everything in this home. For example, we shall laugh over disagreement, we shall laugh over whoever wants to come in-between us, we shall laugh over complaints about each other, we shall laugh over our lack, we shall laugh over the devil – we will turn everything into laughter in this relationship. We will never take serious offence in our relationship, neither are we going to let it dictate how we relate to each other.

10. We shall always pray together and share prayer points together. We will arrange certain days when we will pray and fast for our home.

11. We shall never miss church services in this home. We will get involved in church activities. We and our children will not be nominal Christians.

B. INDIVIDUAL DECISIONS TO MAKE:

The individual partner must make personal decisions such as the following, in order to avoid or come out of strife in the marriage.

1. I shall resist the devil always, in accordance with *James 4:7:* *"Submit yourselves therefore to God. Resist the devil, and he will flee from you."*

   When the devil puts wrong words in my mouth to say to my spouse, I shall refuse.

   When the devil tells me to defend myself against my spouse, I shall refuse to do it. I will tell the devil that God is my defence.

   When the devil tells me to insult my spouse so as to let him or her know that I am not a fool, I shall refuse the suggestion.

2. I shall personally pursue peace in this home, in accordance with *Romans 12:18: "If it be possible, as much as lieth in you, live peaceably with all men."*

   Even when my spouse is ready for war and strife, I shall go for peace.

3. Pray *Galatians 5:22-23* into your life and that of your spouse, always: *"But the fruit of the Spirit is love, joy, peace, longsuffering, gentleness, goodness, faith, meekness, temperance: against such there is no law."*

   Ask God for the grace to exhibit this fruit of the Spirit in your marriage.

It is my prayer that God will journey with you in your marriage, in Jesus' name.

Prayer

Father, please overthrow today, any form of attack of the enemy on the peaceful co-existence between me and my spouse.

Father, please remove now any form of sorrow the enemy has added to your blessings in my marriage.

May the fire of God destroy every evil inheritance in my life that is still active today, in Jesus' name.

Spirit of disorder, I cast you out of my home and send you to hell without returning, in Jesus' name.

I decree that the work of the Holy Spirit shall not cease in my home, in Jesus' name.

I refuse to perform any assignment the enemy has given me against my spouse, in Jesus' name. I shall not be a channel of destruction to my spouse.

In the name of Jesus Christ, I command the fire of God to destroy any form of demonic trap holding my marriage in stagnancy.

I refuse to cooperate with my spouse in anything that would destroy our marriage, in Jesus' name.

Father, let your fire destroy any altar of marital complication erected against my home, in Jesus' name.

Father, overthrow any evil prophet ministering failure against my marriage, in Jesus' name.

8
Co-operative Faith

"*Now faith is the substance of things hoped for, the evidence of things not seen.*"
Hebrews 11:1

Faith is an important ingredient required to receive blessings and help from God. This is true for both an individual and a group of individuals.

Co-operative faith is when two or more people join their faith together to achieve a common purpose. This is usually to strengthen their position concerning their expectations.

In many situations, the husband and wife may join their faith together to trust God for a common need or individual needs. These could be the fruit of the womb, a new job, financial improvement, healing for a sick partner, etc. In such a situation, the faith level of each spouse becomes very important to the success of their common expectations. If the faith of one of the spouses crumbles, it may have a negative impact on that of the other partner. It is therefore very important that the spouse is able to quickly detect when the faith level of his or her partner is faltering.

The devil is a promoter of unbelief, and he will attempt to lure into unbelief and doubt either of the spouses that are jointly

THE ENEMY OF *Marriage*

trusting God for certain blessings in their home. Satan loves to attack the faith of people.

Case study: Abraham and Sarah

"And, behold, the word of the LORD came unto him, saying, This shall not be thine heir; but he that shall come forth out of thine own bowels shall be thine heir. And he brought him forth abroad, and said, Look now toward heaven, and tell the stars, if thou be able to number them: and he said unto him, So shall thy seed be. And he believed in the LORD; and he counted it to him for righteousness."

Genesis 15:4-6

In these Bible verses, God promised the family of Abraham and Sarah a son. Abraham believed God. The two spouses started exercising co-operative faith regarding the promise of God.

"Now Sarai Abram's wife bare him no children: and she had an handmaid, an Egyptian, whose name was Hagar. And Sarai said unto Abram, Behold now, the LORD hath restrained me from bearing: I pray thee, go in unto my maid; it may be that I may obtain children by her. And Abram hearkened to the voice of Sarai. And Sarai Abram's wife took Hagar her maid the Egyptian, after Abram had dwelt ten years in the land of Canaan, and gave her to her husband Abram to be his wife. And he went in unto Hagar, and she conceived: and when she saw that she had conceived, her mistress was despised in her eyes."

Genesis 16:1-4

In the above story, Sarah ran out of faith and she started putting pressure on Abraham to accept her suggestion that came from doubt. Abraham agreed and slept with Haggai.

This is an attack on co-operative faith in marriage.

Lessons from Abraham and Sarah

A. Sarah

1. Sarah started her conversation by attacking God (who Abraham had been trusting for a child): *"And Sarai said unto Abram, Behold now, the LORD hath restrained me from bearing..." (Genesis 16:2).* Here Sarah directly blames God, making Him responsible for her barrenness.

   The spirit of doubt always opposes God, painting God as the root cause of problems. Be alert when your spouse begins to talk against God concerning what the two of you are trusting God for. It is a sign that his or her faith is crumbling.

2. She spoke politely and with respect to Abraham: *"And Sarai said unto Abram, Behold now, the LORD hath restrained me from bearing: I pray thee..." (Genesis 16:2).* Sarah began her conversation respectfully. She used the words "Behold" and "I pray thee". The politeness was intended to draw Abraham into supporting her unbelief. You are likely to give attention to a polite approach because it sounds godly, though, the spirit behind it may not be of God.

   Do not be deceived when your spouse presents a negative, doubting opinion to you in a very polite manner. It is to draw you into doubting God. It is an evidence that his or her faith is collapsing, regarding what the two of you have been trusting God for.

3. Sarah expressed uncertainty: *"And Sarai said unto Abram, Behold now, the LORD hath restrained me from bearing: I pray thee, go in unto my maid; it may be that I may obtain children by her..." (Genesis 16:2).*

   She used the words "may" and "may be", meaning perhaps. These are a sign of gambling. She was indirectly telling

THE ENEMY OF Marriage

Abraham: let us give it a try. That is, there is no promise of success. This is because her suggestion did not come from God. Uncertainty is of the devil – the agent of doubt. People who act based on uncertainty usually use it as an excuse to justify themselves, in case the result of their attempt is negative. It is a protection in case of failure.

Be aware when your partner suggests an act that is based on uncertainty and gambling. It is evidence that his or her faith is crumbling. God does not gamble, and He does not work in darkness.

4. Sarah politely gave a word of instruction: *"And Sarai said unto Abram, Behold now, the LORD hath restrained me from bearing: I pray thee, go in unto my maid; it may be that I may obtain children by her. And Abram hearkened to the voice of Sarai"* (Genesis 16:2).

Sarah did not give Abraham any chance of dialogue. She gave him a word of instruction. She did not ask for Abraham's opinion on her view. If she had given room for Abraham's opinion and time for him to think, he might have spoken a word of faith that would have frustrated her unbelieving plan. Be wary when your spouse pushes you to act urgently against what the two of you have been trusting God for. It could be that a spirit of doubt has taken over his or her spirit.

5. She worked out the plan herself: *"And Sarai Abram's wife took Hagar her maid the Egyptian, after Abram had dwelt ten years in the land of Canaan, and gave her to her husband Abram to be his wife"* (Genesis 16:3).

This verse shows that Sarah worked out the plan by herself; she gave Haggai to Abraham. She did not wait for Abraham to do it. Because the idea was from Sarah, the execution would surely come from her. When the faith of your partner is disintegrating regarding your family, trust in God, you may be bombarded with lofty ideas and promises from your partner to do it alone. Be alert.

B. ABRAHAM

The following could be seen as faults on the part of Abraham in the way he responded to Sarah's suggestion:

1. He did not remind Sarah of God's promises. When Sarah came to him with her suggestion that was contrary to God's will, Abraham could have reminded her of God's promise concerning the same issue. This might have 'opened her eyes'. But instead, Abraham kept quiet, as if God had not spoken about the promise of a son. When your spouse comes with an opinion that contradicts God's promise, you should bring the promise of God to his or her remembrance.

2. He never expressed his own opinion. When Sarah came to him with her opinion, Abraham should have also expressed his own opinion. If he had done that, it may have brought to light the secret work of the spirit of doubt in the family. When your spouse expresses unbelief, you must express faith. Do not keep quiet in the face of doubt.

3. He did not oppose Sarah when she blamed God. This probably gave Sarah more courage to press forward with her evil suggestion. Whenever your spouse speaks against God, you must not keep quiet. It is your responsibility at that moment to reject blaming God or making God responsible for the family problem.

4. He heeded the voice of Sarah. Abraham listened attentively to Sarah's suggestion. He considered it and found it credible to accept. When your spouse comes with a suggestion that is contrary to what God has told you, never obey it. Instead, let your spouse know that the devil is at work.

C. BOTH ABRAHAM AND SARAH

The common faults in the marriage of Abraham and Sarah were:

1. Lack of constructive dialogue. It seems as if the first to suggest anything in the family of Abraham was always considered right. Even in *Genesis 12:11-13*, when Abraham suggested lying, Sarah failed to oppose him. The same thing happened in *Genesis 16:1-4* when Sarah suggested that Abraham should sleep with Haggai. While it is good to operate in unity, it is also good to encourage constructive dialogue in marriage. Let every suggestion be scrutinised before taking action. This will help to expose any impending danger. The Word of God should be used as a standard to weigh any suggestion from either spouse.

2. Unequal access to information. It is revealed in *Genesis 12, 13 and 15* that God always talked to Abraham. That is, Abraham alone received most of the revelation from God. This implies that Sarah depends on second-hand information through Abraham. This suggests that if Abraham fails to pass the information correctly to Sarah, it may put Sarah at a disadvantage. In your marriage, promote total openness. Let both partners have the same access to family matters.

Let both of you grow together in faith. Serve God together, obey God together, attend the same church, pray together and encourage each other to love God more and more. This is the sure way to frustrate the attacks of the devil on co-operative faith in your marriage.

May God expose and frustrate every secret work of the devil in your marriage.

Every seed of doubt in any area of my marriage, die now in Jesus' name.

Every evil manipulation operating in my home, die to your root now in Jesus' name

Any evil hand orchestrating troubling circumstances in my home, wither now in Jesus' name.

Power that disunites a couple, you shall fail in my marriage, in Jesus' name.

Whatever inside of me or my partner that works against our relationship with God, die now in Jesus' name.

Father, let your fire fall to consume the seed of marital uncertainty in my life, in Jesus' name.

Any attack of the enemy against my faith in God shall fail, in Jesus' name.

Father, let the blood of Jesus silence any spirit ministering lies into my mind and that of my spouse, in Jesus' name.

Father, let angels overthrow any form of work of darkness in my home, in Jesus' name.

In the name of Jesus Christ, Father, drive away any form of evil wind that would blow against my home.

9

Jezebel Spirit

"*But there was none like unto Ahab, which did sell himself to work wickedness in the sight of the LORD, whom Jezebel his wife stirred up.*"

1 Kings 21:25

Jezebel was the wife of King Ahab. Their marriage teaches us much about the operation of a controlling spirit, which we can call a Jezebel spirit, and exposes how a spouse can be manipulative.

Jezebel manipulated Ahab to do as she wished. This happened throughout the time that they lived together as a couple. You need to be aware of the operation of this Jezebel spirit, so as to prevent it from invading your marriage. You should be able to detect when one of you has come under the evil influence of a Jezebel spirit.

In many marriages, spouses manipulate each other into wrong decisions that bring disaster into their home. A Jezebel spirit is of the devil. It should be confronted and cast out of the home.

Characteristics of a Jezebel spirit

Whoever comes under the operation of a Jezebel spirit will manifest the following characteristics:

1. A Jezebel Spirit Worships Her Self-Will

A person under the influence of this spirit believes only in his or her own opinion and expects other people to surrender to his or her view. This is to gain control over those people. A Jezebel spirit considers her will to be the best and so it must be done. If you always exalt only your will in the marriage and expect your spouse to always submit to it, without any consideration for his or her view, it is likely that a Jezebel spirit is operating in your life.

In *2 Samuel 24:1-4*, David instructed Joab to count the people. Despite the advice of Joab not to do it, David ensured that his will prevailed. A Jezebel spirit does not tolerate a conflicting will or view – her will must be done in all situations.

2. A Jezebel Spirit is Self-Dependent

"And Jezebel his wife said unto him, Dost thou now govern the kingdom of Israel? Arise, and eat bread, and let thine heart be merry: I will give thee the vineyard of Naboth the Jezreelite."

1 Kings 21:7

Due to her arrogant nature, this spirit depends on her own strength, wisdom and knowledge. She is confident of herself. She does not seek counsel, neither from man nor God. Jezebel spoke arrogantly to her husband: "I will give thee…" This spirit likes using the word 'I' to reveal her self-dependent nature. If you are self-dependent and have no regard to your spouse's position in all your ways, a Jezebel spirit is likely to be ruling your life.

Marriage is about sharing together the dreams, vision, ideas, wisdom, knowledge, strength, possessions and every other thing God has given to you as a human being. Spouses are expected to depend on each other as they live together. This is the essence of marriage – it is a life shared together, not a life lived alone.

3. A JEZEBEL SPIRIT APPROPRIATES POWER TO HERSELF

"Then Jezebel sent a messenger unto Elijah, saying, So let the gods do to me, and more also, if I make not thy life as the life of one of them by tomorrow about this time."

1 Kings 19:2

This spirit does not seek approval from any authority or person. She encroaches into the territory of another person without seeking their approval. Jezebel spoke to Elijah as if she was a king. She claimed power for herself. She acted as if she was a king and did not even seek the approval of her husband before her action.

If you act in your marriage as an 'alpha and omega' – always doing everything, it is likely you have a Jezebel spirit. There are certain responsibilities that are meant for the husband, and others that are meant for the wife. As a married person, you must respect the individual responsibilities in the marriage. If you want to do everything without your spouse's approval, your spouse may start feeling that you consider him or her useless in the marriage, and that is probably why you want to do everything. When an individual is allowed to function in a certain capacity, it helps the person to develop and discover one's hidden potential. Avoid actions that may intimidate your spouse and make him or her feel worthless in the marriage. Respect your spouse's functions and responsibilities. Do not grab all the power and keep all the roles for yourself.

4. A JEZEBEL SPIRIT IS POWER CONSCIOUS

"And Jezebel his wife said unto him, Dost thou now govern the kingdom of Israel? Arise, and eat bread, and let thine heart be merry: I will give thee the vineyard of Naboth the Jezreelite."

1 Kings 21:7

This spirit always expects people to recognise her authority. She loves announcing her position.

Jezebel reminded her husband that he is the king of the land. This is how she also thought of herself. She is power conscious and power driven.

She just loves to be in a position of authority. If you are always fighting for power in your marriage, it is likely that you have a Jezebel spirit. Jezebel loves to have more power so that she can gain control of people. The more power she has the more she will be able to do as she wishes.

In such a home, in any little discussion, the one with more power in the marriage will always remind and ask the other partner questions such as: "Do you know who you are talking to?" This indirectly reminds the other partner to recognise his or her position in their relationship. This is common where such a partner takes the major responsibilities in the marriage, such as organising the finances. Many marriages are in crisis today because of in-fighting between the spouses for more power.

5. A JEZEBEL SPIRIT EXERCISES CONTROL OVER THE CHOICES OF PEOPLE

"Now the Lord is that Spirit: and where the Spirit of the Lord is, there is liberty."

2 Corinthians 3:17

She wants to determine the future, dreams, vision and destiny of people. She likes telling people what their tastes should be. She will not allow people to exercise liberty concerning their destiny. If you like dictating everything to your spouse, it is likely that you have a Jezebel spirit. Do not turn your spouse into a robot. Allow him or her to make choices in life by him or herself.

Let your spouse enjoy the liberty God has given to him or her. You may counsel your spouse, but it should not be a rule that he or she can't make a choice in any situation without your approval.

6. A JEZEBEL SPIRIT IS A SEDUCER

"Now the Spirit speaketh expressly, that in the latter times some shall depart from the faith, giving heed to seducing spirits, and doctrines of devils…"

1 Timothy 4:1

A Jezebel spirit influences people to act against their will or better judgement. She will manipulate their minds until they fall into errors they would not have fallen into naturally. She exerts pressure and entices people to do her will.

If your influence on your spouse makes him or her depart from the faith and do things your spouse would not have done naturally, you are likely to have a Jezebel spirit. In your marriage, you are to promote faith and godliness in the life of your spouse, not the other way round.

7. A JEZEBEL SPIRIT HATES CRITICISM

"And the king of Israel said unto Jehoshaphat, There is yet one man, Micaiah the son of Imlah, by whom we may enquire of the LORD: but I hate him; for he doth not prophesy good concerning me, but evil. And Jehoshaphat said, Let not the king say so."

1 Kings 22:8

No matter how logical a criticism appears, a Jezebel spirit does not tolerate it. She gets angry when she hears view and opinions that oppose her own. To her, criticism is evidence of hatred.

If you live with a person who has a Jezebel spirit, you must always accept his or her views and opinions, otherwise you will

THE ENEMY OF Marriage

be considered an enemy. This is because she is under the illusion that she is wiser than anybody, especially her partner.

The king of Israel hated Micaiah because Micaiah prophesied bad things about him. A person with a Jezebel spirit hates negative views of him or herself. Whoever does not promote his or her foolish ways is considered an enemy. If this describes you, you may be suffering from the attack of a Jezebel spirit.

8. A JEZEBEL SPIRIT IS SELF-STYLED

"But covet earnestly the best gifts: and yet shew I unto you a more excellent way."

1 Corinthians 12:31

This spirit does not copy anyone. She creates her own ways of doing things. She is always claiming to be original because of her proud nature. Even if other people's ways are better than hers, she will still cling to her own that will never work.

Are you self-styled? Do you sometimes submit to the views and ideas of your spouse, or do you just cling to yours even when it is clear it is inferior?

There is a time to copy good things from others. Your spouse has potentialities that you may not have. Do not let a Jezebel spirit rob you of the blessing of the strengths that are in your spouse that you lack.

9. JEZEBEL SPIRIT IS CRITICAL OF OTHER PEOPLE

"And Eliab his eldest brother heard when he spake unto the men; and Eliab's anger was kindled against David, and he said, Why camest thou down hither? And with whom hast thou left those few sheep in the wilderness? I know thy pride, and the naughtiness of thine heart; for thou art come down that thou mightest see the battle."

1 Samuel 17:28

This spirit faults and opposes people. The plan is to gain control of them.

Eliab, the brother of David, manifested the spirit of Jezebel in his dealing with David. He attacked the mind of David with an accusation. His plan was to make David feel irresponsible. If David should fall into such trap, he would lose his self-esteem and develop a guilty conscience. This would enable Eliab to bring David down emotionally and gain control of him and his mind.

If you always attack your spouse and find fault in whatever he or she does, you may be suffering from a Jezebel spirit. Avoid using guilt as a weapon of control over your spouse.

10. A JEZEBEL SPIRIT CRAVES A GOOD REPUTATION

"Notwithstanding I have a few things against thee, because thou sufferest that woman Jezebel, which calleth herself a prophetess, to teach and to seduce my servants to commit fornication, and to eat things sacrificed unto idols."

Revelation 2:20

She likes praising herself, magnifying her own strength, ability and success. This spirit loves boasting and improving her reputation so as to gain confidence from people and use it to control them.

A person of a Jezebel spirit will advertise herself and rain praises on her own deeds. She sometimes gives herself titles that are intended to show her authority or power. Like the Jezebel in Revelation, she may call herself a prophetess to win people's confidence and seduce them into following her. She just wants recognition that she can use to dominate others.

If you like fighting for your reputation and using it to oppress your spouse, you are likely to have Jezebel spirit.

11. A JEZEBEL SPIRIT IS DOMINEERING IN CONVERSATION

"For when they speak great swelling words of vanity, they allure through the lusts of the flesh, through much wantonness, those that were clean escaped from them who live in error."

2 Peter 2:18

She always wants to have the last word in every conversation. This is because she believes she has better ideas than other people.

If you are domineering in conversation, you may notice that your spouse soon goes quiet when both of you are engaged in a discussion. Your spouse will soon find that arguing with you is a waste of time because you are overbearing, not allowing him/her to properly share opinions and points of view.

A domineering spirit is one of the characteristics of a Jezebel spirit. It creates difficulties in communication and builds a wall of separation between spouses.

12. A JEZEBEL SPIRIT PREFERS WEAKER ASSOCIATES AND FRIENDS

This is because such people are easy to manipulate and they don't pose any challenge in a relationship. A Jezebel spirit does not like a challenger. She will avoid strong opponents who can argue their position effectively. She prefers to marry someone who will be easy to manipulate.

In *2 Samuel 15:10-12*, Absalom surrounded himself with people that would always agree with his rebellion against his father, David. These are people he considered useful for his evil operation. If you don't like engaging your spouse in discussion because you are afraid of losing the argument, it maybe because you have a Jezebel spirit.

If you prefer that your spouse shouldn't further his/her education and career because you are afraid that it will boost his/her confidence and position, and will mean you can't control your spouse anymore, it could be because you have a Jezebel spirit. You will need to repent.

13. A JEZEBEL SPIRIT IS UNGOVERNABLE

It is difficult to exercise authority over a person who has a Jezebel spirit. She can't submit to any authority. She can only be at peace with you if you allow her to rule over you. If you are ungovernable to your spouse, it could be because you have Jezebel spirit.

14. A JEZEBEL SPIRIT IS FULL OF SELFISHNESS AND FAVOURITISM

She can only support an authority that will favour her. She can never give her support to any authority or purpose unless it is to her advantage. Such a person will not support family plans unless they are to his/her benefit. She is selfish and does not care if a purpose is good or evil so long as it favours her. She will reject people who do not go along with her ideas, and will influence other people to do the same as her.

Do you manipulate your spouse to hate what you hate and like what you like? If so, maybe you have a Jezebel spirit.

15. A JEZEBEL SPIRIT IS A SCHEMER

She is efficient in plotting the downfall of other people. She knows how to pretend and use fake humility to pull people down. In *2 Samuel 15:1-6*, Absalom used fake humility, concerns and sympathy to draw Israelites towards himself in order to pull his father down. Do you scheme against your spouse with fake concerns? If yes, you need to get rid of a Jezebel spirit from your life, otherwise your home can't have genuine peace.

16. A JEZEBEL SPIRIT IS CRAFTY

"That she called unto the men of her house, and spake unto them, saying, See, he hath brought in an Hebrew unto us to mock us; he came in unto me to lie with me, and I cried with a loud voice: and it came to pass, when he heard that I lifted up my voice and cried, that he left his garment with me, and fled, and got him out."

Genesis 39:14-15

She is a man-user. She knows how to draw people's attention and support to her side.

In the above story, the wife of Potiphar used words to draw sympathy from other household members to support her against Joseph. She used words such as 'us' to indicate that the so-called bad treatment she received from Joseph was against all the members of the household. This was to make other people share her cause. Jezebel uses a variety of methods to manipulate people for her selfish purposes.

If this kind of habit describes you, you need to change before it destroys your relationship with your spouse – and with others. When your spouse discovers your trick, he/she will feel angry with you and may get to a point where he/she can no longer take it anymore.

17. A JEZEBEL SPIRIT USES THE DIVIDE-AND-RULE STRATEGY

This is to prevent unity among people. Divided people are easy to use for the selfish gain of the manipulator. Unity frightens a Jezebel spirit, so she prefers to turn people against each other. A spouse who suffers from this spirit may create division among relatives of her spouse, turning their hearts against each other. She may also do the same among the couple's children.

18. A JEZEBEL SPIRIT ATTACKS THE MIND

"Let no man despise thy youth; but be thou an example of the believers, in word, in conversation, in charity, in spirit, in faith, in purity."

1 Timothy 4:12

She can attack the mind of people in order to gain control of them. She can cause guilt, condemnation, accusation, fault-finding, etc. She can even quote Bible verses to make you feel guilty. She can instil an inferiority complex into your mind by emphasizing your faults, weaknesses, inadequacies and errors. This is to make you feel incapable and lose self-confidence.

A Jezebel spirit can also threaten you, using the weapon of fear to capture and gain control of you. This spirit despises other people.

If this describes you, you might have dehumanised your spouse and taken away his/her self-esteem. Such a spouse will not be able to manifest their hidden potential for the benefit of their family. You need to repent.

19. A JEZEBEL SPIRIT HAS AN EVIL TONGUE

"Now Tobiah the Ammonite was by him, and he said, Even that which they build, if a fox go up, he shall even break down their stone wall."

Nehemiah 4:3

She knows how to discredit and ridicule what she hates.

Due to hatred and jealousy, Tobiah discredited the walls Nehemiah was building. He described the walls as being feeble, using an exaggeration to make his point. He did this to weaken the resolve of the builders and gain control of their strength. A Jezebel spirit is an expert in exaggerating the poor condition of what she hates.

THE ENEMY OF *Marriage*

Do you have an evil tongue that mocks and makes fun of others, discrediting what you hate? If your words are always discouraging your spouse and make him/her abandon something good whenever you speak about it, then you have an evil tongue. You need to repent.

20. JEZEBEL SPIRIT IS REVENGEFUL

People suffering from this spirit don't forgive. They seek revenge or wish evil on those who offend them. This spirit believes that if it can't control a person, that person is not fit to live. The person affected by a Jezebel spirit becomes very bitter and offended when his/her spouse refuses to be manipulated.

You are suffering from this spirit if you are seeking revenge for an offence committed against you by your spouse, or whenever your spouse refuses to be used by you for your selfish gain. If you rejoice when your spouse suffers evil, you have a Jezebel spirit. If you wish your spouse evil due to an offence or bitterness, you are suffering from a Jezebel spirit. You will need to repent, otherwise your actions may attract the wrath of God.

21. A JEZEBEL SPIRIT ALWAYS DEMANDS AN APOLOGY

The person suffering from this spirit always believes that people have wronged her but she has never wronged anybody. She always believes that people owe her an apology. You are suffering from a Jezebel spirit if you always attack your spouse for wrongdoing and demand an apology, yet you never believe you have ever wronged your spouse.

22. A JEZEBEL SPIRIT PERVERTS LEADERSHIP STRUCTURES

She does not respect or have regard for any hierarchy of authority. She always wants to deal with the most senior in an organisation, thinking she can succeed in gaining control of the person. If she manages to rule over the leader then all the subordinates automatically come under her dominion.

A spouse suffering from this spirit has no regard for the authority of his/her partner. He/she will not obey or respect any boundary set up in their relationship. If you can't obey rules you jointly set up with your spouse, it maybe because you are suffering from a Jezebel spirit.

23. A JEZEBEL SPIRIT ADULTERATES THE TRUTH

This is another attempt to gain control of people. She contaminates the truth in order to cause confusion. This opens the door for her to manipulate the confused people. If you always make your spouse confused due to your manipulative comments, you need to fight a Jezebel spirit ruling over your life. If you breed confusion and take advantage of your spouse when he/she is confused, a Jezebel spirit is living inside you. Get rid of it.

24. A JEZEBEL SPIRIT TAKES ADVANTAGE OF PEOPLE'S WEAKNESSES.

She is alert and watches people, hoping to see them make an error or mistake and then use it as a weapon of oppression to manipulate them. She gathers evil and damaging information about people and uses it against them.

If you use your spouse's secrets or other weaknesses to fight him/her, you are under the control of a Jezebel spirit. You need to stop this evil action before it destroys your marriage.

25. A JEZEBEL SPIRIT TURNS PEOPLE INTO PUPPETS

She wants to determine people's behaviour, reasoning and action. She does not allow people to act independently. She is a controller. If you are always controlling your spouse and want him/her to act and behave your way, you have a Jezebel spirit. Don't turn your spouse into a puppet. Allow your husband or wife to make his/her own choices. You can help each other to become better, but don't try to turn your partner into your puppet.

26. A JEZEBEL SPIRIT EXERTS EVIL PRESSURE

She exerts evil pressure on people to force them to conform to her expectations and gain control of them.

In *Judges 16:16-17*, Delilah pressurises Samson to do what she wants him to do. If you always exert pressure on your spouse in order to get your own way, you may be suffering from a Jezebel spirit.

Bribing, blackmailing or even just persistent nagging are not appropriate ways of making your spouse conform to your expectations. There are better, godly means you can employ to persuade your spouse. For example, you can present your points in a polite way, with all the necessary facts and figures to convince your spouse to support your point of view. You can also approach God to touch his/her mind concerning the matter. And if he/she doesn't change his/her mind, it may be because your case is unjust or you are the one who is mistaken.

27. A JEZEBEL SPIRIT DENIES HER REAL NATURE

She will never accept that she has a problem. This makes her very difficult to help. She is also unrepentant because she does not believe that she has done anything wrong. This is what makes her very stubborn.

If you see yourself as faultless in every situation, and see no reason for any apology or repentance, it maybe because you are suffering from a Jezebel spirit. If you don't change, this may destroy your marriage. Your spouse may get tired of living with a stubborn and unrepentant person.

28. A Jezebel spirit has unrealistic expectations

This is what makes her unpleasable. She always expects from people, what they can't afford to give. She will set standards for people which she herself can't meet. She will demand from people what she knows is impossible. Nothing satisfies her. If you try to please her, you will wear yourself out.

If nothing from your spouse pleases you, it could be that you have a Jezebel spirit. Do not expect from man what only God can provide.

29. A Jezebel spirit uses what she has, to control other people

If it is a woman, she can use sex as a weapon to oppress her husband. She will deny her husband sex until he gives in to what she wants.

If it is a man and the main breadwinner, he can use money or any other material things to oppress his wife. He may demand that his wife should do certain things for him before he can give her the financial support she desperately needs. This is wrong. If this describes you, you need to stop it now before it destroys your home.

God did not give you any blessing or possession so that you can use it as a weapon of oppression against your spouse.

30. A Jezebel spirit is a potential murderer

She can kill with her tongue by destroying a person with her words. She can also kill with her bad treatment of other people. If you suffer from this spirit, you need to repent before it uses you to kill your marriage. Nobody wants to live the rest of his/her life with somebody possessed by a Jezebel spirit.

Father, overthrow any power/spirit/personality violating your purpose for my home, in Jesus' name.

Father, root out of my home today any tree you have not planted, in Jesus' name.

Father, whoever wants to scatter what you are building in my home, overthrow them today, in Jesus' name.

Every evil influence upon me causing me to misbehave in my marriage, I use the blood of Jesus to cancel you in my life, in Jesus' name.

You spirit of Jezebel, you shall not prosper in my life and in my spouse's life, in Jesus' name.

Any area of my marriage that the enemy has captured, I take it back today, in Jesus' name.

Every dictate of the enemy over my marriage shall fail, in Jesus' name.

I command any power or spirit delaying my marital breakthrough and good testimony to enter into captivity, in Jesus' name.

Any satanic representative standing between me and my spouse, I uproot you by fire, in Jesus' name.

Seed of stubbornness, die out in me now, in Jesus' name.

10

Spiritual Warfare in Marriage

"*Therefore shall a man leave his father and his mother, and shall cleave unto his wife: and they shall be one flesh.*"
Genesis 2:24

This verse indicates that marriage is a union between a man and a woman, to live together as husband and wife.

Genesis 3:1 describes the attack of Satan on the first couple: *"Now the serpent was more subtil than any beast of the field which the Lord God had made. And he said unto the woman, Yea, hath God said, Ye shall not eat of every tree of the garden?"*

But the operation of Satan against humanity is ongoing; just as he has attacked man in the past, so he is still doing it today: *"Be sober, be vigilant; because your adversary the devil, as a roaring lion, walketh about, seeking whom he may devour" (1 Peter 5:8).*

Spiritual warfare in marriage means battling against demonic interference in the affairs of the home. Marriage is a war when Satan or his demons invade the home.

It should be noted that in the beginning, Adam and Eve had no problem in their relationship until Satan interfered. The same principle is still valid today. Most of the serious problems in marriage have satanic connections.

THE ENEMY OF *Marriage*

If you can easily or quickly detect Satan's hand at work, you will be able to defeat him in your marriage before the damage is done. But if you still believe that your spouse or children are the major cause of your marital problems, when it is really Satan, you will not be able to defeat Satan and his manoeuvres in your marriage.

Demonic invasion

You need to understand the stage at which Satan's demons get involved in the affairs of a home. For Satan to invade a marriage, certain conditions need to be in place, created either by one of the partners or both. Satan does not have the power to force himself on the affairs of a home, but he is clever enough to take advantage of the messes we make by ourselves.

In *John 6:70-71,* Jesus told His disciples that one of them would betray him: *"Jesus answered them, Have not I chosen you twelve, and one of you is a devil? He spake of Judas Iscariot the son of Simon: for he it was that should betray him, being one of the twelve."*

Up until this time, Judas was operating without any satanic involvement. He was under the influence of his own weaknesses. But Judas loved money, as is revealed in *John 12:4-6*: *"Then saith one of his disciples, Judas Iscariot, Simon's son, which should betray him, Why was not this ointment sold for three hundred pence, and given to the poor? This he said, not that he cared for the poor; but because he was a thief, and had the bag, and bare what was put therein."*

Judas was under the influence of the love of money. It seems it was his main motive for betraying Jesus. He went to those looking to arrest Jesus, with the intention of making money by promising them that he would deliver Jesus into their hands: *"And Judas Iscariot, one of the twelve, went unto the chief priests, to betray him unto them. And when they heard it, they were glad, and promised to give him money. And he sought how he might conveniently betray him"* (Mark 14:10-11).

At this stage, Judas was still in control of himself, though the love of money was influencing him from inside. Satan was not involved in the matter at this stage. But Judas refused to repent before it was too late. Jesus made it clear on several occasions, in the presence of Judas, that one of the disciples would betray him. For example: *"The Son of man indeed goeth, as it is written of him: but woe to that man by whom the Son of man is betrayed! Good were it for that man if he had never been born"* (Mark 14:21).

In this verse, Jesus even gave a warning about the terrible consequences for whoever betrayed him. Yet, Judas refused to repent. At this stage, Judas was still operating alone. He was under his self-will, not Satan's control. So Judas could still have repented.

It should be noted that even if Jesus was to be betrayed, it is not stated in any of the gospels that it had to be Judas. Jesus would definitely be betrayed, but the person Satan used had to be somebody who had the seed of Satan inside him.

What was that seed? Judas's greed and love of money. You need to have some sin at work in you for Satan to succeed in using you for any operation.

Judas's weakness for money made him a prime candidate for Satan to use to betray Jesus. Having missed all the opportunities to repent, he was primed and ready when *"the prince of this world cometh"* (John 14:30).

So Satan took over Judas: *"Then entered Satan into Judas surnamed Iscariot, being of the number of the twelve"* (Luke 22:3).

The greed in Judas opened the door for Satan. Now matters were out of Judas's hands; he had lost the ability to control his behaviour towards Jesus. Satan would now be in charge of his thoughts and actions, leading him to betray Jesus. Repentance was now impossible for Judas. He would only be in a position to come to his senses and repent after Satan had left him – when he had finished the assignment Satan had for him. And that's exactly what happened:

"Then Judas, which had betrayed him, when he saw that he was condemned, repented himself, and brought again the thirty pieces of silver to the chief priests and elders, saying, I have sinned in that I have betrayed the innocent blood. And they said, What is that to us? See thou to that. And he cast down the pieces of silver in the temple, and departed, and went and hanged himself."

Matthew 27:3-5

Satan left him alone once the job was completed. Judas now realised his error, but it was too late. He had missed several good opportunities for genuine and timely repentance that would have saved Jesus.

The following lessons can be learned from Judas's story:

1. Truly, Satan hates marriage and he wants to destroy it. But it is not mandatory that Satan must use either of the partners to destroy their marriage. However, if any of the partners make themselves available to be used by Satan, then he will seize the opportunity. Satan has no particular plan to use certain individuals, but whoever makes himself or herself available will be used. Do not make yourself a candidate for Satan to use to destroy your home.

2. Don't give Satan a foothold. Avoid sin and any unrighteousness. Sin is a thing of Satan, and if you have it inside you, you are offering an open door for Satan to come in and destroy your home. Examples of such sin could include: anger, hatred, irritation, greed, selfishness, arrogance, deception, abuse, etc.

3. Satan is closely monitoring you, looking for the best time to strike. You are the one who creates the best time for Satan

to attack your marriage, by your actions. You are inviting a satanic invasion into the affairs of your home when you promote the things of Satan (sin).

4. Delaying repentance is dangerous. The more you put off repenting, the harder it will be to repent. The best time to repent of all wrongdoings is as soon as you realise your error. Never delay repentance when you find yourself convicted about a sin. Never ridicule a genuine correction. Never seek to justify your sinful behaviour. Do not make your partner the excuse for your mistake. Take personal responsibility for your wrongdoing, irrespective of whether your partner has contributed to it or not.

5. Avoid gambling with the destiny of your marriage. You are gambling with the destiny of your marriage when you indulge in wrong habits that have the potential to destroy your home. The consequences may be unimaginable.

6. Face the reality of your vulnerability. You must realise that when Satan gets involved in the affairs of a home, the partners are likely to lose control of the marriage. You must understand that when Satan enters into you through your error, you will not be able to control yourself over that matter until Satan comes out of you.

7. Regret is evidence that you once sold yourself out to Satan. Learn from every action you have embarked-on in the past that brought you regret. It could be an opportunity for you to guard against a regret that will come with more severe consequences in the future.

8. Satan is a murderer. When he uses a person against himself, he sends into the person, a heart of regret and thoughts of death that come through a lack of self-forgiveness. Be quick

to forgive yourself for whatever big mistake you might have committed, and learn how to avoid repeating the same thing in the future. Judas did not forgive himself because his repentance was of the world, not of God. Don't kill yourself or hate yourself because of an error you committed, nor for allowing Satan to influence you, nor for the wrong motivation that led you to commit sin.

"For godly sorrow worketh repentance to salvation not to be repented of: but the sorrow of the world worketh death."

2 Corinthians 7:10

Signs of demonic interference in the affairs of a home include the following:

1. JUSTIFICATION TO DISOBEY GOD

Whenever either one or both of the spouses agree to disobey God, their marriage is at war and there is the possibility of demonic invasion or influence.

One of the names of Satan is the tempter: "And when the tempter came to him, he said, If thou be the Son of God, command that these stones be made bread" (Matthew 4:3).

A tempter is the person who lures somebody to do wrong things, providing opportunities to sin. He makes sinful things look good. A tempter gives convincing reasons to somebody to disobey God's commands.

Whenever you or your spouse feel a strong justification to do a wrong thing, you are likely to be under the influence of Satan – the tempter.

"Now the serpent was more subtil than any beast of the field which the Lord God had made. And he said unto the woman, Yea, hath God said, Ye shall not

eat of every tree of the garden? And the woman said unto the serpent, We may eat of the fruit of the trees of the garden: But of the fruit of the tree which is in the midst of the garden, God hath said, Ye shall not eat of it, neither shall ye touch it, lest ye die. And the serpent said unto the woman, Ye shall not surely die: For God doth know that in the day ye eat thereof, then your eyes shall be opened, and ye shall be as gods, knowing good and evil. And when the woman saw that the tree was good for food, and that it was pleasant to the eyes, and a tree to be desired to make one wise, she took of the fruit thereof, and did eat, and gave also unto her husband with her; and he did eat."

Genesis 3:1-6

In this story, Satan assumed the role of marketing manager, trying to convince Adam and Eve that they should buy into his disobedience. He told them the benefits of disobeying God.

Be aware that Satan builds his kingdom on deception. He deceives people to trust him and not God.

Whenever you have strong reasons to do wrong things, you are likely to be under demonic influence and invasion. Whenever you feel you have a good reason to do what is against the Word of God, you are being deceived.

Psalm 119:89 says: *"For ever, O Lord, thy word is settled in heaven."* That is, what God has said remains valid irrespective of the situation of your life. If you choose to act against the Word of God based on your personal justification, you are under the deception of Satan. *Isaiah 5:20* says: *"Woe unto them that call evil good, and good evil; that put darkness for light, and light for darkness; that put bitter for sweet, and sweet for bitter!"* You call evil good when you have your own justification for doing things that God has condemned.

2. PROLONGED DISUNITY

A marriage is at war when it faces continual disunity between the spouses. Satan loves to attack the unity of a home. He loves to cause separation and disagreement.

He uses different tactics to disunite couples. Prolonged bitterness or anger opens the door to disunity. If the couple refuse to forgive each other and harbour bitterness in their hearts, Satan will take advantage of such a situation to invade the home.

In *Matthew 12:30,* Jesus said: *"He that is not with me is against me; and he that gathereth not with me scattereth abroad."*

Satan can be described as the agent of scattering. He loves to scatter people, to disunite them. He disunites couples by turning their hearts against each other. He does that by sowing lies into their hearts.

In *Matthew 13:25* Jesus described Satan in this way: *"But while men slept, his enemy came and sowed tares among the wheat, and went his way."* So another description of Satan is sower of tares (weeds).

The tares in the relationship could be lies. If the wife lies to the husband and the husband lies to the wife, the couple will find it difficult to trust each other.

Whenever you notice that you and your spouse are finding it very difficult to trust each other, the devil is likely to be at work in your marriage.

It should be noted that Satan promotes disunity in order to make the couple fall either individually or collectively.

3. A CYCLE OF AFFLICTION

Your home is under attack when you or your spouse goes from one trial to another, and then another, and it never seems to stop. If you are living in such a cycle of affliction, it may be Satan's doing.

2 Corinthians 2:11 teaches us that Satan is out to *"get an advantage of us,"* so we should not be *"ignorant of his devices"*.

Spiritual Warfare in Marriage

Satan is an exploiter and a schemer. An exploiter is the person who takes advantage of the situation and uses it to achieve a personal ambition.

Every home faces the normal challenges of life that God permits to build up our faith. But if a couple does not handle those challenges very well, Satan can take advantage of them to lead the couple into another difficulty. He will use their bad attitude to the problem to create another problem for them. The couple are now facing more than one problem at the same time.

A biblical example of this is in *1 Samuel 1:1-6: "Now there was a certain man of Ramathaimzophim, of mount Ephraim, and his name was Elkanah, the son of Jeroham, the son of Elihu, the son of Tohu, the son of Zuph, an Ephrathite: And he had two wives; the name of the one was Hannah, and the name of the other Peninnah: and Peninnah had children, but Hannah had no children. And this man went up out of his city yearly to worship and to sacrifice unto the LORD of hosts in Shiloh. And the two sons of Eli, Hophni and Phinehas, the priests of the LORD, were there. And when the time was that Elkanah offered, he gave to Peninnah his wife, and to all her sons and her daughters, portions: But unto Hannah he gave a worthy portion; for he loved Hannah: but the LORD had shut up her womb. And her adversary also provoked her sore, for to make her fret, because the LORD had shut up her womb."*

In this story, Hannah was the first wife of Elkanah, but the Lord had shut her womb. Barrenness in the culture of Israel was considered a curse, but Hannah's infertility was not a curse but a temporary trial from God. It was God who was responsible for her situation. But instead of responding to Hannah's childlessness in faith, Elkanah had taken matters into his own hands and married a second wife called Peninnah.

The first problem of the family of Elkanah was that Hannah had not had a child – a challenge from God. Unfortunately,

THE ENEMY OF Marriage

Satan took advantage of Hannah's infertility to bring the family into a polygamous situation, so the family moved from the issue of barrenness to the problem of polygamy. They now started having a real marital crisis – caused by Penninah. The presence of Penninah at home became a second affliction in the life of Hannah.

Elkanah had not handled the trial well. He allowed the cultural interpretation of Hannah's case to control him. He yielded to cultural and family pressure, and as a result, the home moved from crisis to crisis. The devil was definitely in the background, manipulating the mind of Elkanah, using culture and family members.

Whenever you notice that it seems as if your home just moves from one crisis to the next, then the enemy could be at work. You need to arise against the attacker of your home – the devil.

I pray that any power sponsoring crises in your marriage shall die today, in Jesus' name.

4. DIFFICULTY HONOURING VOWS

When a couple finds it difficult to honour a vow they have made, it is likely that the enemy is at work – especially when it becomes a tradition in their home.

2 Corinthians 11:3 uses another name for Satan – the serpent: *"But I fear, lest by any means, as the serpent beguiled Eve through his subtilty, so your minds should be corrupted from the simplicity that is in Christ."*

When Satan shows up as a serpent, he injects poison into people's minds. He corrupts people's thinking so that they drop the reason for honouring the vow they had made. This defeats the original thought that brought the idea of the vow into being. The couple start justifying the change of position regarding their vow.

Sometimes, agitation of the mind could be the factor that enables the devil to lure the couple into dishonouring their vow, either individually or as a couple.

In many homes today, it is very difficult for them to honour vows.

For example, if a husband and wife make a vow never to fight in the presence of their children, it is not long before their minds get distracted and they forget their vow and break it. If a couple make a vow never to treat each other in a certain wrong way anymore, then very soon Satan will cleverly organise a situation that will make them forget all the good reasons for making such a vow, and they will go back to behaving as they did before the vow. *"As a dog returneth to his vomit, so a fool returneth to his folly" (Proverbs 26:11).*

Whenever you notice that it is always difficult for you and your spouse to honour a vow, it is likely that the enemy is at work.

You must know that one thing will lead to another. People who never honour vows never grow. Such people move round the circle of the same old negative story time and time again – the same argument, the same reason for fighting, the same accusation, the same counter-accusation, etc.

I pray that every spirit that has arrested peace in any area of your home shall enter into captivity today and forever, in Jesus' name.

5. DOUBT THAT LEADS TO ACTING IN UNBELIEF

Whenever you or your spouse develop doubt towards God's faithfulness, such that it leads you to act in unbelief, Satan is likely to be at work.

It is one thing to have doubt; it is another thing to back it with action. Satan is an enemy of God. He hates God and always hinders whatever is of God. He prevents people from putting their faith and trust in God.

THE ENEMY OF Marriage

An example is in *Acts 13:7-11:* "*... the deputy of the country, Sergius Paulus, a prudent man... called for Barnabas and Saul, and desired to hear the word of God. But Elymas the sorcerer (for so is his name by interpretation) withstood them, seeking to turn away the deputy from the faith. Then Saul, (who also is called Paul,) filled with the Holy Ghost, set his eyes on him. And said, O full of all subtilty and all mischief, thou child of the devil, thou enemy of all righteousness, wilt thou not cease to pervert the right ways of the Lord? And now, behold, the hand of the Lord is upon thee, and thou shalt be blind, not seeing the sun for a season. And immediately there fell on him a mist and a darkness; and he went about seeking some to lead him by the hand.*"

In this story, a human agent of Satan was trying to prevent people from putting their faith in God. Satan always attempt to hinder people from trusting God. He attacks their minds.

In *Genesis 15:4*, the Lord promised Abraham a son: *"And, behold, the word of the lord came unto him, saying, This shall not be thine heir; but he that shall come forth out of thine own bowels shall be thine heir."*

But in *Genesis16:1-10*, due to doubt, Sarah put pressure on Abraham to sleep with Haggai. The couple chose to help themselves concerning the promise of God for their lives. The spirit of doubt was at work in their marriage, unknowingly to them. They eventually committed an act that was in line with their unbelief. Whenever your doubt leads you into an action of unbelief, Satan is likely to be at work.

In the same way as Abraham and Sarah, maybe you and your spouse have been trusting God for certain blessings, but when you face a delay, you agree to help things along yourself. If so, it is likely that Satan is working through you. Satan is putting a lie into your mind. Satan knows that doubt could abort the promises of God, so he will attempt to make you doubt God's promises for your home.

6. EVIDENCE OF AN EVIL PATTERN

When you notice any pattern of evil behaviour in your home that you can trace back to previous generations, it is probably a sign that Satan is at work.

Psalm 91:3 reveals another name for Satan – a fowler: *"Surely he shall deliver thee from the snare of the fowler, and from the noisome pestilence."*

A fowler is someone who hunts wild birds for food, using traps to catch his prey. Satan the fowler is an evil hunter, using many different traps to capture human beings. One of the traps he uses is a generational curse or evil pattern. In this trap, he ensures that every child or person born into a home carries the evil seeds that have been planted in past generations.

Whenever you notice a repetition of negative events in your home that can be traced back through your family tree or that of your spouse, then, your home is under attack.

In *Matthew 15:13*, Jesus said: *"Every plant, which my heavenly Father hath not planted, shall be rooted up."*

The plant here symbolises whatever is contrary to the will of God. Every tree God has not planted was planted by Satan's will. Whenever you notice a tree God has not planted in your home, then your home is being attacked by your enemy.

For example, in some families, the tree God has not planted is marital unfaithfulness. Members of such a family always find it difficult to stay faithful for a long time. Adultery is a common thing. It has a long history in the family.

In some other families the tree may be anger. They can't keep relationships together because of a hot temper. That is their family pattern.

THE ENEMY OF *Marriage*

In some homes, it is abuse. If you marry into such a family, expect some kind of abuse. They will always be able to come up with good excuses for maltreating their spouses. This is because a curse is running in the family.

In some other families, it is pride. They consider other fellow human beings as inferior. Every child raised in such a family was brought up under the influence of the spirit of pride. If you marry someone from such a home, you may be treated badly.

In some families, it is untimely death. They don't live long. They may never reach a certain age. Other trees God has not planted in some families include hardship, many kinds of failure, such as career failure, business failure, etc.

All these are an indication that a curse is running in that family and that Satan is in control of certain areas of the family's affairs. Unless somebody rises against it, the curse will continue to run in the lives of other family members.

I pray that every kingdom set over your life that is not of God shall be removed today, in Jesus' name.

7. ACTIVITY OF THE SPIRIT OF BELIAL

"Now the sons of Eli were sons of Belial; they knew not the Lord."

1 Samuel 2:12

The spirit of Belial is the spirit that takes over the life of a child and tailors his path through life to become a worthless and wicked son or daughter.

Satan loves to take over children and make them his own.

When you notice the activity of the spirit of Belial in your child, Satan is at work.

In *Matthew 13:4*, Jesus told a parable where *"some seeds fell by the way side, and the fowls came and devoured them up..."* This shows another name for Satan – a fowl or bird. Birds eat seeds that are exposed. Any seed that is not protected or covered is open to the attack of a bird.

Satan is a thief, and whatever is left unattended or unprotected will be stolen by him. A child that is left to him or herself will be taken over by Satan.

If you are so busy that you have no time for your child, Satan will go behind your back to take control of your child. Perhaps this is the reason why Satan loves keeping parents busy, so that they have no time with their children. He is then able to take over their children's lives.

1 Samuel 2 records that Eli was a prophet. He was very busy with the work of the temple, so perhaps he had no time to teach and train his sons. As a result, Satan was able to fill the gap left by Eli and take over the lives of his sons.

You need to create time for training your children in the ways they should go in life. If you fail in this responsibility, you will open a door to Satan to take over your children's lives.

8. THE WEEDS

"Another parable put he forth unto them, saying, The kingdom of heaven is likened unto a man which sowed good seed in his field: But while men slept, his enemy came and sowed tares among the wheat, and went his way. But when the blade was sprung up, and brought forth fruit, then appeared the tares also. So the servants of the householder came and said unto him, Sir, didst not thou sow good seed in thy field? From whence then hath it tares? He said unto them, An enemy hath done this. The servants said unto him, Wilt thou then that we go and gather them up?"

Matthew 13:24-28

In this parable, a man sowed good seed in his field but later discovered weeds among the crops. The enemy sowed the weeds.

Weeds or tares in a field retard the growth of the farmer's plants, defeating the best efforts of the farmer to improve the standard of his crop. Weeds compete with crops for food. They will not allow the crops to have the full enjoyment of the blessings of the farmer and the earth. They restrict the quality of life of the crops, devouring nutrients that should have been for the crops. They siphon life out of the good plants.

It is likely that Satan is at work in your home when you discover the activity of a devourer. When you notice that resources are being siphoned out of your home, it is likely that the enemy is at work. When you notice that all the good efforts you are making to improve the situation in your home are not yielding the expected result, it is likely that enemy is at work. Satan is a devourer. He can siphon blessings out of a place. He can cause the loss of good resources. He can hinder the manifestation of good results. He can frustrate our best efforts.

If you notice that you are working like an elephant but eat like an ant, you may need to x-ray your life situation. Financial unfaithfulness to God can open the door to the activity of a devourer. Ignoring warnings could also attract weeds into the affairs of a home. If you notice that all your good efforts to make the situation better in your home are not working, you will need to take it to God in prayer. Weeds will not let seeds grow healthily.

9. Disorder

The presence or involvement of Satan in any affairs is marked by disorder. Disorder means chaotic and confusing situations, and it means to be out of control.

Spiritual Warfare in Marriage

When the situation in your home is haphazard or chaotic for a long time, your home is at war. Prolonged confusion brings a lack of direction and leads to error. When you and your spouse are engulfed in confusion, the enemy is at work. Confused people are vulnerable. You must fight disorder. Don't allow Satan to cause your home to be upside down.

Disorder could also mean a physical condition in which there is a disturbance of normal functioning. Disorder will not let the husband operate as a husband or the wife function as a wife. It distorts the proper arrangement of a situation. Where there is disorder, there is a lack of respect or honour. Disorder produces everything that is abnormal, both spiritually and materially. It takes away discipline and orderliness. It also produces perversion, and it takes away the sound mind that God gave you when you became born again *(2 Timothy 1:7)*.

Ecclesiastes 10:7 says: *"I have seen servants upon horses, and princes walking as servants upon the earth."* This is the reversal of the normal hierarchy. Things can also be upside down in some homes. If you see a home where the children seem to rule the roost, rather than the parents, or if the wife 'wears the trousers', it is a sign of disorder. If this describes your marriage or home, a spirit of disorder is at work.

Things get twisted when disorder is at work. Nothing is straight in a place of chaos. Here, what is supposed to yield a good result will yield a poor result. A journey that should take a year may take many years, due to disorder.

God never dwells in a place of disorder. The more you allow disorder in your home, the more you will squeeze God out of your home, and the more you will feel the absence of God in your family.

10. EVIL DOMINION

This is a situation whereby you desire to do something good but later discover that what you did was wrong. That is, you want to do the right thing but end up doing something else. This could also be the situation with your partner. You may have jointly agreed to do something good, but at the point of execution, you both did the opposite.

The Apostle Paul had this problem himself: *"For that which I do I allow not: for what I would, that do I not; but what I hate, that do I" (Romans 7:15).*

It is very possible to have every good intention but fail miserably when it comes to the point of putting it into action. It is also possible for a couple to decide to embark on a certain project, but when the time comes, they divert the resources into a different, wasteful exercise. If this frequently happens, it is very likely that the enemy is at work. You will need to rise against the evil dominion exerted by Satan over you, or you and your partner.

The good news is that spiritual warfare in marriage is winnable. *James 4:7* says: *"Submit yourselves therefore to God. Resist the devil, and he will flee from you."*

That is, bring your entire self under the dominion of God. When you allow God to rule your life in every area, Satan will not have his way. You will be able to resist Satan. When Satan attempts to influence your thoughts and actions, you will be able to refuse him.

This is very necessary *"because your adversary the devil, as a roaring lion, walketh about, seeking whom he may devour"*, so we need to *"be sober, be vigilant..." (1 Peter 5:8).*

To be vigilant means not being careless. It also means watching carefully for possible danger or difficulties. A vigilant person will live conscious of the fact that Satan is not far away and that the days are full of evil. This should make you avoid any volatile situation that could open a door to Satan's involvement. Be very careful not to give ground to Satan in all your dealings with your spouse.

Only the full armour of God guarantees your victory against Satan: *"Put on the whole armour of God, that ye may be able to stand against the wiles of the devil" (Ephesians 6:11).*

Half obedience will fail you. Half righteousness will not work. Faith in God today and doubt tomorrow will not produce a good result. You must always be alert. You must always do and act rightly. You must always be good to your spouse. You must always be ready for combat against the forces of hell. Only this guarantees your continual victory.

Prayer

Father, arise and scatter all the enemies of your good purpose for my marriage.

Father, arise and frustrate every evil counsel concerning my home, in Jesus' name.

Father, arise and terminate every warfare in my marriage, in Jesus' name.

Father, arise and destroy every evil work in any area of my home, in Jesus' name.

Father, you are a man of war; fight for my home today, in Jesus' name.

Evil dominion set over my marriage – collapse now, in Jesus' name.

Father, shut the door against any way in which Satan is manifesting in the affairs of my home, in Jesus' name.

Every chain of the enemy binding me or my spouse, fire of God destroy it now – in Jesus' name.

I use the blood of Jesus to rub off every satanic mark on my home, right now in Jesus' name.

I decree that there shall be no more war, no more trouble, no more attack and no more anxiety in my home, in Jesus' name.

11

Brokenness

Brokenness means a process whereby the pride in a man is removed to make him rely on God. It makes us always rely on God for everything. It is the humbling of the proud.

A broken man is the one whose pride in his power has been broken: *"And I will break the pride of your power; and I will make your heaven as iron, and your earth as brass" (Leviticus 26:19).*

For you to be successful in marriage, you will need to be broken by the Holy Spirit. The pride in you needs to be totally removed, otherwise, you will not be able to dwell with your spouse under the same roof. You will only be opening the door to satanic attack in your home.

Marriage requires a lot of maturity, and only broken people can adequately meet the requirement. The more broken you are (as revealed by the level of your humility), the better your chances of being successful in marriage.

How do you know a broken person?

1. A BROKEN PERSON IS MATURE

Such a person can tolerate and endure a lot of things in life. He/she is rarely engaged in an argument that will lead to strife. A broken person has matured so much that he or she knows the boundary in everything.

A broken person has endurance: *"Therefore I endure all things for the elect's sakes, that they may also obtain the salvation which is in Christ Jesus with eternal glory"* (2 Timothy 2:10).

Only a broken man like the writer Timothy, Paul, can endure all things, including persecution, insults, hardship, mockery, etc. Such a person easily overlooks offence.

If we are broken, we rely on God to handle all situations for us. We let God talk and act on our behalf. We do not act in our own strength but in God's.

2. A BROKEN PERSON IS REAL

Broken people never pretend. They will never claim to be what they are not. This is because their reliance is on God, not on themselves.

Despite all the anointing on him, King David did not feel ashamed to say that he was weak: *"And I am this day weak, though anointed king; and these men the sons of Zeruiah be too hard for me: the LORD shall reward the doer of evil according to his wickedness"* (2 Samuel 3:39).

Are you real or still living a life that is not yours?

3. A BROKEN PERSON IS HUMBLE

This is because the self in broken people has died. They exalt others above themselves. They rely on God to exalt them.

Numbers 12:3 says that *"Moses was very meek, above all the men which were upon the face of the earth".* Moses was so meek and humble because he was a broken man. He never believed himself to be superior to others, despite his position as leader and prophet. He never made himself an idol for people to worship.

You need meekness to live well with your spouse, otherwise, even without realising it, you will demand that he/she should start worshiping you. If this is the case, a revolt is imminent.

4. A BROKEN PERSON DOES NOT DEMAND A REWARD

A broken man relies on God to reward him for whatever good things he has done.

God told Abram that he was his reward: *"After these things the word of the LORD came unto Abram in a vision, saying, Fear not, Abram: I am thy shield, and thy exceeding great reward" (Genesis 15:1).*

A broken man does not seek payback for help given to somebody. He expects a reward from God, not man. Whatever good you might have done to your spouse, let God reward you. Don't use that to control him or her.

5. A BROKEN PERSON DOES NOT DEMAND RECOGNITION OR RESPECT

Broken people only seek God's praise.

It was God who magnified Joshua in the eyes of his people: *"On that day the LORD magnified Joshua in the sight of all Israel; and they feared him, as they feared Moses, all the days of his life" (Joshua 4:14).*

Joshua did not seek Israel's approval. It was God who showed people that Joshua had his anointing. Joshua did not promote himself, telling others about his power.

Do not demand recognition from your spouse. You must earn respect by your actions, and then God will honour you in the sight of your spouse.

6. A BROKEN PERSON DOES NOT FIGHT FOR POSITION

Such a person relies on God to exalt him.

THE ENEMY OF *Marriage*

It was God that touched the hearts of the people to make David king: *"So all the elders of Israel came to the king to Hebron; and king David made a league with them in Hebron before the LORD: and they anointed David king over Israel"* (2 Samuel 5:3).

Though, David had been anointed as king by God's prophet many years earlier, he waited for God to organise his enthronement in His own way. He did not scheme and manipulate people to become king.

Do not make your spouse agree with you over every matter. Let God bring him or her conviction.

7. A BROKEN PERSON DOES NOT SEEK REVENGE

"And when David heard that Nabal was dead, he said, Blessed be the LORD, that hath pleaded the cause of my reproach from the hand of Nabal, and hath kept his servant from evil: for the LORD hath returned the wickedness of Nabal upon his own head. And David sent and communed with Abigail, to take her to him to wife."

1 Samuel 25:39

A broken person relies on God to punish the evildoer. David did not take revenge for the evil done to him by Nabal; God did it for him. Do not return evil for evil against your spouse. Romans 12:20 says that instead of seeking revenge, "if thine enemy hunger, feed him; if he thirst, give him drink: for in so doing thou shalt heap coals of fire on his head". Doing good to those who have done evil to us is not only right, it may also prick their conscience and give God the chance to convict them of wrong.

Let God fight for your cause. Vengeance is mine, says the Lord. If you are doing right, He will fight your battle.

8. A BROKEN PERSON DOES NOT SEEK SUPPORTERS

Broken people rely on God to bring them supporters. They do not manipulate or cajole people to support them.

1 Chronicles 12:22 says: *"For at that time day by day there came to David to help him, until it was a great host, like the host of God."* Helpers came to David on their own accord. He did not bribe them neither did he cajole them. It was God that touched their hearts to serve him.

Allow God to steer your life: *"The king's heart is in the hand of the LORD, as the rivers of water: he turneth it whithersoever he will" (Proverbs 21:1).*

Do not recruit your parents or relatives to take your side against your spouse. Avoid seeking other people's support to justify your position on any marital matter. Let God do it. Let him vindicate you. If you are in the right, He will.

9. A BROKEN PERSON DOES NOT FIGHT FOR BLESSINGS OR POSSESSIONS

Broken people rely on God to give them what belongs to them.

In *Genesis 13*, Abraham and Lot had to choose where to settle. Lot relied on his own wisdom, while Abraham relied on God. Lot chose the land that seemed good to him. But God chose for Abraham.

Avoid fighting your spouse over money or possessions. Let God decide for you. God is a God of justice. He will give you all you need if you trust Him.

10. A BROKEN PERSON DOES NOT DEFEND HIMSELF/HERSELF

Broken people rely on God to defend them. They don't respond to blackmailing or wrong accusations. God is their focus.

In *Daniel 3:16-18*, Shadrach, Meshach and Abednego risked their lives on God. They said to the king: *"O Nebuchadnezzar, we are not careful to answer thee in this matter. If it be so, our God whom we serve is able to deliver us from the burning fiery furnace, and he will deliver us out of thine hand, O king. But if not, be it known unto thee, O king, that we will not serve thy gods, nor worship the golden image which thou hast set up."*

These three Hebrews did not defend themselves before the king. They were not looking for human approval. Stop defending yourself against your spouse's arguments, if he or she is in the wrong. Let God defend you.

11. A BROKEN PERSON EXHIBITS THE FRUIT OF THE SPIRIT

Finally, the more you exhibit the fruit of the Spirit, the more you will make it difficult for Satan to use you to make trouble in your marriage.

Galatians 5:22-23 lists the fruit of the Spirit as *"love, joy, peace, longsuffering, gentleness, goodness, faith, meekness, temperance: against such, there is no law."*

Remember that Satan needs your help to destroy your marriage and it is your weaknesses that provide the help that he needs. If you have been broken by God and all those weaknesses Satan needs are no longer in you, then it will be impossible for Satan to destroy your marriage. Your home will become untouchable to Satan.

May God make you stronger than your enemy, in Jesus' name.

Prayer

Father, root out of me today, whatever inside of me that resists your good purpose for my marriage, in Jesus' name.

Any fire of marital failure burning inside of me or my partner, I command you to be quenched today by the fire of the Holy Spirit, in Jesus' name.

Father, create in me a clean heart and renew a right spirit within me, in Jesus' name.

Father, take out of me every spirit that is not of you, in Jesus' name.

Every remnant of old things (bad habits, thoughts and imagination) that still remain in me, Father, wash them away today with the blood of Jesus.

I receive from the Lord today, the grace to operate with the mind of Jesus, in His name.

I shall not operate in the destiny of another man, but I shall operate in my own destiny, in Jesus' name.

Any power hindering the smooth flow of the river of love in my marriage, fall and die now, in Jesus' name.

Whatever in me that is fuelling trouble in my home, die out of me now, in Jesus' name.

Father, I thank you that you will make my marriage glorious, in Jesus' name.

BOOKS FROM THE SAME AUTHOR

Journey to the Next Level

The New Creature

Building a Glorious Home:
A Pathway to a Successful Marriage

The Winning Formula

Words that Heal

This book, and all other aforementioned books, from the same author, are available at Christian bookstores and distributors worldwide.

They can also be obtained through online retail partners such as Amazon or by contacting the author at the address below:

Contacts:

21-23 Stokescroft

Bristol BS1 3PY

United Kingdom

E-mail:

kkasali@yahoo.com

Telephone:

+44 (0)7727159581

www.ingramcontent.com/pod-product-compliance
Lightning Source LLC
Chambersburg PA
CBHW071927290426
44110CB00013B/1503